Contents

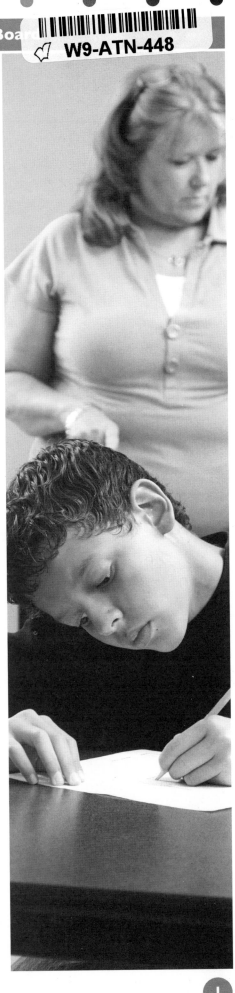

Dear Students,

The private schools you'll find in books and on television may be interesting, but the real world of independent schools is even more amazing. You're reading this guide right now because you think that an independent school might be right for you, and you're ready for one of the first steps—taking the SSAT.

This book will introduce you to the SSAT, the test format, and what to expect on test day. It contains sample tests that closely resemble the actual test you'll be taking, plus test preparation tips to help you do your best on the SSAT.

The Official Guide to the SSAT gives you:

- An explanation of an admission test
- Descriptions of the test sections
- Test-taking strategies
- Plenty of sample questions to practice
- Two full-length practice tests
- Information about how to interpret scores
- A registration and test-day checklist

What won't you find here? Shortcuts, tricks, or gimmicks ("when in doubt, C wins out"). This is the only book that contains practice questions and actual practice tests written by SSAT test writers and with the official test-taking strategies to allow you to do your best. There are some valuable hints that can help you stay on track and maximize your time. But when it comes down to it, getting familiar with the test format and scoring, studying specific content covered on the test, and taking practice tests is the best way to prepare for the SSAT.

The path ahead will be exciting, and you'll probably learn a lot about yourself on the way. We wish you the best as you prepare for and take the SSAT and find and apply to a school that will change your life. This book can help you get there.

The Secondary School Admission Test Board (SSATB)

Dear Parents,

Congratulations on your decision to explore an independent school education for your child! For more than 50 years, the SSAT has been the standard in admission testing for the world's best independent schools. We know that the process of taking the SSAT can be fraught with concern and distress, but it needn't be. The SSAT is one important step on the road to an independent school education—one which should be taken seriously, but should not cause undue anxiety.

The results of admission testing, while integral to an application, are just one of many factors considered by admission officers when determining if your child and their schools make a great match. The degree of emphasis placed on scores depends on the school and on other information, such as transcript and teacher recommendations. For the vast majority of schools, students with a wide range of SSAT scores are admitted.

Here are a few questions that admission officers contemplate when reviewing an applicant's scores:

- Are the scores consistent with the student's academic record?
- Do the scores highlight areas of academic strength or weakness?
- How do these scores compare with those of other students in the applicant pool?
- How do these scores compare with students who have enrolled over the last few years?

As a parent, you have a central role to play in helping your child to succeed in the school application process by supporting them to keep the SSAT in perspective. Schools are most interested in finding out who your child is.

There are a multitude of sources, both on- and off-line, that promise to prepare your child for the SSAT and increase his/her test score. SSATB does not endorse any test preparation company, individual, or book; even those classes given by our member schools are not sanctioned by our organization. Written by our test development team, this guide was created to support your student's preparation efforts with legitimate information, test-taking strategies, and practice tests. We encourage you to use this guide as your official source for SSAT preparation.

Finally, we encourage you to use the ssat.org web site not only to register your child for the test, but also to access information about the independent school application process and search for schools that are the right fit for your child and your family.

We hope this *Official Guide to the SSAT* will help to make your family's experience of testing and applying to independent school a successful and enjoyable one.

Good luck!

Heather Hoerle

Heather Hoerle
Executive Director

Chapter One: What is the SSAT?

What is the Purpose of the SSAT?

The SSAT is designed for students who are seeking entrance to independent schools worldwide. The purpose of the SSAT is to measure the basic verbal, quantitative, and reading skills students develop over time—skills that are needed for successful performance in independent schools. The SSAT provides independent school admission professionals with meaningful information about the possible academic success of potential students like you at their institutions, regardless of students' background or experience.

The SSAT is not an achievement test. Your most recent classroom math test, for example, was probably an achievement test: Your teacher specifically designed it to evaluate how much you know about what has been covered in class. The SSAT, on the other hand, is designed to measure the verbal, quantitative, and reading skills you have acquired, instead of focusing on your mastery of particular course materials.

Further, SSAT tests are not designed to measure other characteristics, such as motivation, persistence, or creativity that may contribute to your success in school.

How is the SSAT Designed?

The SSAT measures three constructs: verbal, quantitative, and reading skills that students develop over time, both in and out of school. It emphasizes critical thinking and problem-solving skills that are essential for academic success.

The SSAT is constructed to be of middle difficulty for those who take the test. In other words, about 50% of the examinees will get the average test question correct. The distribution of question difficulties is set so that the test will effectively differentiate among test takers, who vary in their level of skills.

In developing the SSAT, the SSATB convenes review committees, composed of content experts and independent school teachers. The committees reach consensus regarding the appropriateness of the questions. Questions judged to be acceptable after the committee review are then pretested and analyzed. Questions that are statistically sound are ready to be selected and assembled into test forms.

Is the SSAT Reliable?

The SSAT is highly reliable. The scale score reliability is higher than .90 for both the verbal and quantitative sections, and is approaching .90 for the reading section, which is considered quite high in the educational field.

The SSAT is a Norm-Referenced Test

The SSAT is a norm-referenced test. A norm-referenced test interprets an individual test-taker's score relative to the distribution of scores for a comparison group, referred to as the *norm group*. The SSAT norm group consists of all the test takers (same grade/gender), who have taken the test for the first time on one of the Standard Saturday or Sunday SSAT administrations in the USA and Canada over the past three years.

The SSAT reports percentile ranks, which are referenced to the performance of the norm group. For example, if you are a boy in the 6th grade, and your percentile rank on the March 2012 verbal section is 90%, it means that 90% of all the other 6th grade boys' (who have taken the test for the first time on one of the Standard Saturday or Sunday SSAT administrations in the USA and Canada between 2008 and 2011) scores fall below your scale score. The same scale score on the SSAT may have a different percentile rank from year to year, and the SSAT percentile ranks should not be compared to other tests in the same testing year because each test is taken by a different group of students.

In contrast, a criterion-referenced test interprets a test-taker's performance without reference to the performance of other test takers. For example, your percent correct from a classroom math test is 90%, because you answered 90% of the questions correctly. Your score is not referenced to the performance of anyone else in your class.

It is important to remember that the SSAT norm group is a highly-competitive group. You are being compared to all the other students (same grade/gender) who are taking this test for admission into independent schools— some of which can be the most selective schools in the country. Most important to remember is that the SSAT is just one piece of information considered by schools when making admission decisions and, for the vast majority of schools, students with a wide range of SSAT scores are admitted.

The SSAT is a Standardized Test

Although each year several different SSAT forms are administered, the SSAT is administered and scored in a consistent or standard manner. The reported scores or scale scores are comparable and can be used interchangeably, regardless of which test form students take. A scale score of 500 on the June 2013 Middle Level verbal section, for example, has the same meaning as the scale score of 500 from the December 2012 Middle Level verbal section, although the forms are different. The score interchangeability is achieved through a statistical procedure, referred to as *score equating*. Score equating is used to adjust for minor form difficulty differences, so that the resulting scores can be compared directly.

Standard also refers to the way in which tests are developed and how tests are administered. Regarding test development, a standard process for writing, testing, and analyzing questions—before they ever appear on a live test— is used. Further, SSAT provides precise instructions to be followed by qualified and experienced test administrators from the moment you are admitted to the test center until the time of dismissal. Any deviations from the uniform testing conditions are reported by the test administrator in writing to SSATB. Of course, a student with a school-documented need may apply for special testing accommodations, but the processes and procedures for the test's administration remain the same.

Should I Guess on the SSAT?

The answer is: It depends. You must first understand how the test is scored.

When your test is scored, you will receive one point for each correct answer. You will <u>lose</u> one quarter of a point for each incorrect answer. You will not receive or lose points for questions that are not answered. If you guess, try guessing only when you can eliminate one or more answer choices as wrong.

A few things to keep in mind:

Keep moving. Do not waste lots of time on a question that is hard for you. If you cannot answer it, flag or make a note of it in your test book and go on. Go back to it later if there is time.

Earn as many points as you can on easy questions. You receive one point for each correct answer, no matter how hard or easy the questions are. Do not throw away points on questions you know how to answer through careless errors.

Check your answer sheet. Mark your answers in the correct row on the answer sheet. Be especially careful if you skip questions.

Chapter Two: About the Middle Level SSAT

The SSAT is a multiple-choice test that consists of verbal, quantitative (math), and reading comprehension sections. The Middle Level SSAT is for students in grades 5-7, and provides admission officers with an idea of your academic ability and "fit" in their schools. The best way to ensure that you perform as well as you possibly can on the SSAT is to familiarize yourself with the test. Familiarity with the format of the test and review of practice questions will make your test-taking experience easier. You'll feel more comfortable with the test and be able to anticipate the types of questions you'll encounter.

This chapter will introduce you to the kinds of questions you'll see on the Middle Level SSAT and the best ways to approach them. The Quick Questions that accompany each section will give you some practice, before you tackle the two practice tests that appear later in the book. In this chapter, we also will provide the test-taking strategies that students should know when they take the Middle Level SSAT. The bonus from these test-taking strategies is that they also can help you perform better on the tests you take in school!

> The best way to make sure you perform as well as you can on the SSAT is to become familiar with the test—a little prep work.

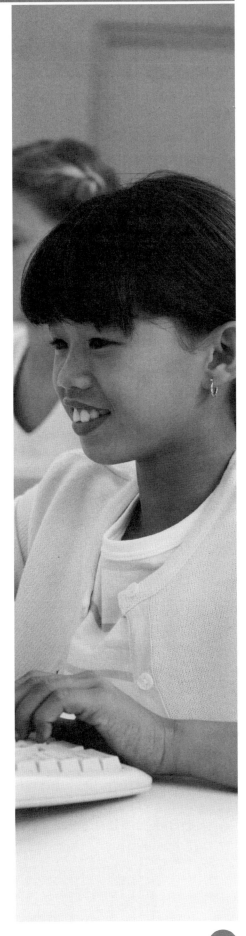

The Middle Level Test Consists of FIVE Sections:

1. A Writing Sample

Number of questions: You will have a choice between two creative story starters.

What it measures: This gives admission officers a feel for how well you write and organize your ideas.

Scored section: No, but it is forwarded to the schools you have selected to receive your score reports.

Time allotted: 25 minutes

Topics covered: Students are given a choice between two creative story starters.

2. A Quantitative (Math) Section

Number of questions: 50, broken into two parts

What it measures: Your ability to solve problems involving arithmetic, elementary algebra, geometry, and other concepts

Scored section: Yes.

Time allotted: 30 minutes for the first 25 questions, and 30 minutes for the final 25 questions

Topics covered:

Number Concepts and Operations

- Arithmetic word problems (including percent, ratio)
- Basic concepts of addition, subtraction, multiplication, and division
- Estimation
- Rational numbers
- Sequences and series
- Frequencies

Algebra (elementary concepts of algebra)

- Properties of exponents
- Algebraic word problems
- Equations of lines
- Patterns
- Absolute value

Geometry/Measurement

- Area and circumference of a circle
- Area and perimeter of a polygon
- Volume of a cube, cylinder, box
- Pythagorean theory and properties of right, isosceles, equilateral triangles
- Properties of parallel and perpendicular lines
- Coordinate geometry
- Slope

Data analysis/probability

- Interpretation (tables, graphs)
- Trends and inferences
- Probability

3. A Reading Comprehension Section

Number of questions: 40

What it measures: Your ability to read and comprehend what you read

Scored section: Yes.

Time allotted: 40 minutes

Topics covered:

Reading passages generally range in length from 250 to 350 words and may be taken from the following:

- Literary fiction
- Humanities (biography, art, poetry)
- Science (anthropology, astronomy, medicine)
- Social studies (history, sociology, economics)

Questions related to the passage may ask you to:

- Recognize the main idea
- Locate details
- Make inferences
- Derive the meaning of a word or phrase from its context
- Determine the author's purpose
- Determine the author's attitude and tone
- Understand and evaluate opinions/arguments
- Make predictions based on information in the passage

4. A Verbal Section

Number of questions: 60 — 30 synonyms and 30 analogies

What it measures: Vocabulary, verbal reasoning, and ability to relate ideas logically

Scored section: Yes.

Time allotted: 40 minutes

Topics covered: This section covers word similarities and relationships through synonyms and analogies.

5. The Experimental Section

Number of questions: 16

What it measures: The SSATB is continuously creating new tests to make sure the questions are reliable, secure, and acceptable for the SSAT. These questions may be used on a future SSAT.

Scored section: No.

Time allotted: 15 minutes

Topics covered: This section contains six verbal, five reading, and five quantitative questions for you to answer.

Test Overview		
Section	**Number of Questions**	**Time Allotted To Administer Each Section**
Writing Sample	1	25 minutes
Break		5 minutes
Section 1 (Quantitative)	25	30 minutes
Section 2 (Reading)	40	40 minutes
Break		10 minutes
Section 3 (Verbal)	60	30 minutes
Section 4 (Quantitative)	25	30 minutes
Section 5 (Experimental)	16	15 minutes
Totals	167[1]	**3 hours, 5 minutes**

[1]*Of the 167 items including the writing sample, only 150 questions are scored.*

I. The Writing Sample

At the beginning of the test, you will be asked to write an essay in 25 minutes. You'll have a choice between two creative prompts. Your writing sample will be sent to the admission officers at the schools to which you're applying to help them assess your writing skills. This section is not scored by SSATB, and a copy of it is not included in the scores that are sent to your family—unless you choose to purchase a copy of your writing sample to accompany your online score report.

What are the Directions for the Writing Sample Section of the Test?

Schools would like to get to know you better through a story you tell using one of the ideas below. Please choose the idea you find most interesting and write a story using the idea as your first sentence. Please fill in the circle next to the one you choose.

How are the Writing Topics Presented?

The topics are designed to spark your imagination and creativity. They will ask you to start a story based on a phrase such as:

JUST THE FACTS

The Writing Sample

Number of questions:
You will have a choice between two creative story starters.

What this measures:
While not scored, this gives admission officers a feel for how you write.

Scored section:
No, but it is forwarded to the schools you have selected to receive your score reports.

Time allotted:
25 minutes

EXAMPLE

> I put my hand in my pocket and pulled out …
>
> *or*
>
> All I wanted was a glass of water.

This is a chance for you to showcase the unique way you think and write.

Tips for Getting Your Writing Sample Started

Read the topics carefully. Take a few minutes to think about them and choose the one you prefer. Then organize your thoughts before you begin writing (scrap paper for organizing your thoughts will be provided when you test). Be sure that you use a pencil, that your handwriting is legible, and that you stay within the lines and margins. Remember to be yourself and let your imagination soar!

If you want to change what you write, neatly strike through the words you want to eliminate and add the new words so they are legible. Two line-ruled pages will be provided. Don't feel as if you have to fill both pages—just do your best to provide a well-written story.

Practice Writing Samples

This book includes practice writing sample prompts, which can be found at the beginning of the practice tests. Each sample includes directions, a prompt, and an answer sheet similar to the answer sheet you'll receive during the actual test.

> Remember: Your writing sample will not be scored. Schools use the sample to get to know you better through a story you tell.

Writing Sample Test-Taking Strategies

1. While creativity is encouraged, remember that the admission officers in the schools to which you are applying will be reading your writing sample. You want to be sure that your story is appropriate and one that you would not hesitate to turn in for a school assignment.

2. Read both prompts. Take a couple of minutes to think about what you're going to write. You can use your scrap paper to organize your thoughts.

3. Choose a working title for your story. The Middle Level SSAT doesn't require a title, but a working title will help to keep you on track.

4. Get involved in your story. Provide detail, describe emotions, and have fun.

5. Make sure your story has a beginning, a middle, and an end.

6. If there's time, check your writing and correct spelling, punctuation, and grammatical errors.

2. The Quantitative Sections

The two quantitative (mathematics) sections of the Middle Level SSAT measure your knowledge of algebra, geometry, and other quantitative concepts. The words used in SSAT problems refer to mathematical operations with which you are already familiar.

What are the Directions for the Quantitative Section on the Test?

Following each problem in this section, there are five suggested answers. Work each problem in your head or in the blank space provided at the right of the page. Then look at the five suggested answers and decide which one is best.

How are the Quantitative Questions Presented?

Many of the questions that appear in the quantitative sections of the Middle Level SSAT are structured in mathematical terms that directly state the operation you need to perform to determine the best answer choice.

EXAMPLE

> 13, 26, 39, 4◊
>
> In the number pattern above, ◊ =
>
> (A) 6
> (B) 10
> (C) 11
> (D) 12
> (E) 18
>
> **The correct answer is (D).**

Other questions are structured as word problems. A word problem often does not specifically state the mathematical operation or operations that you will need to perform in order to determine the answer. In these problems, your task is to consider carefully how the question is worded, and the way the information is presented, to determine what operations you will need to perform.

EXAMPLE

> Kathy and Donna ran a three-mile race. Kathy jogged the first two miles at 6 miles per hour and walked the last mile at 4 miles per hour. Donna ran the first mile at 10 miles per hour and walked the final two miles at 3 miles per hour. What is the difference between the times taken by the two girls?
>
> (A) Kathy finished the race 3 minutes ahead of Donna.
> (B) Kathy finished the race 4.5 minutes ahead of Donna.
> (C) Kathy finished the race 11 minutes ahead of Donna.
> (D) The two girls finished in the same time.
> (E) Donna finished the race 4 minutes ahead of Kathy.
>
> **The correct answer is (D).**

Quantitative Test-Taking Strategies

1. Read the question/problem carefully.

2. Pace yourself. Try not to spend too much time on one question.

3. Be sure to use the "Use This Space for Figuring" area of your test book to do the scratch work.

4. Always check to see if you have answered the question asked. Circling what's being asked can be helpful, so you don't mistakenly choose the wrong answer.

5. Watch for units of measure. Be sure you know and understand what units of measurement the answer is supposed to be given in.

6. Draw graphics. If you find that a problem is complicated, you can draw a graph, diagram—anything that will allow you to understand what the problem is asking.

7. Remember to mark your answers on the answer sheet! If you solve the question in your answer book and do not mark it on your answer sheet, the answer will not be counted.

Quick Questions

On the following pages, you'll find brief overviews of the Middle Level SSAT math question types you'll encounter on the test. Review each Quick Question description and then complete the questions that illustrate the concept.

Quick Questions: Percentages

Following each problem in this section, there are five suggested answers. Work each problem, then look at the five suggested answers and decide which one is best.

Percent (%) means hundredths or number out of 100, so that $\frac{40}{100} = 40$ percent, and 3 is 75 percent of 4 (because $\frac{3}{4} = \frac{75}{100} = 75$ percent).

---

1. In a class of 25 students, 8 received a grade A on a math quiz. What percent of the students did not receive an A?
   (A) 8%
   (B) 25%
   (C) 32%
   (D) 68%
   (E) 78%

---

2. About 55.2% of the salt in sea water is chloride and 30.4% is sodium. What percent is neither chloride nor sodium?
   (A) 12.6%
   (B) 14.4%
   (C) 28.8%
   (D) 55.8%
   (E) 85.6%

---

3. 82% of the 400 cars in the parking lot are red. How many of the cars are red?
   (A) 82
   (B) 182
   (C) 228
   (D) 328
   (E) 350

---

4. 24% of the houses on Elm Street (12 houses) have gray roofs. 36% of the houses on Elm Street (18 houses) have green roofs. The remaining houses all have black roofs. How many houses have black roofs?
   (A) 10
   (B) 20
   (C) 30
   (D) 50
   (E) 60

Answer Key: Percentages

1. **Answer (D) 68%**

   $\frac{8}{25} = 32\%$ $100\% - 32\% = 68\%$

2. **Answer (B) 14.4%**

   $55.2 + 30.4 = 85.6$ $100\% - 85.6\% = 14.4\%$

3. **Answer (D) 328**

   $.82 \times 400 = 328$

4. **Answer (B) 20**

   $24\% + 36\% = 60\%$ $12 + 18 = 30$ 60% (30 houses) are gray or green.

   $\frac{60\%}{100\%} \times \frac{30}{x}$

   $x = 50$ (total houses)
   $50 - 30 = 20$

Quick Questions: Fractions

A fraction has a numerator and a denominator. The numerator is on top, and the denominator is on the bottom. The numerator is divided by the denominator.

For example: $\frac{1}{2}$ ↔ numerator
↔ denominator

When fractions have the same numerator but different denominators, the one with the larger denominator is smaller.

For example: $\frac{1}{8} < \frac{1}{4}$

Questions 1 and 2 are based on the boxes of cards.

Sandy bought 2 boxes of plain cards containing 20 cards each. She created 27 "thank-you" cards and she kept the remainder as "all occasion" cards.

1. What fractional part were "thank-you" cards?
    (A) $\frac{13}{20}$
    (B) $\frac{13}{40}$
    (C) $\frac{20}{40}$
    (D) $\frac{27}{40}$
    (E) $\frac{30}{40}$

2. What fractional part were "all occasion" cards?
    (A) $\frac{13}{20}$
    (B) $\frac{13}{40}$
    (C) $\frac{20}{40}$
    (D) $\frac{27}{40}$
    (E) $\frac{30}{40}$

3. Give the fraction that represents the shaded part of
    (A) $\frac{2}{5}$
    (B) $\frac{2}{6}$
    (C) $\frac{3}{6}$
    (D) $\frac{2}{3}$
    (E) $\frac{3}{5}$

4. Give the fraction that represents the shaded part of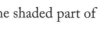
    (A) $\frac{2}{6}$
    (B) $\frac{3}{6}$
    (C) $\frac{4}{6}$
    (D) $\frac{5}{6}$
    (E) $\frac{6}{6}$

5. Give the fraction that represents the shaded part of
    (A) $\frac{2}{8}$
    (B) $\frac{1}{4}$
    (C) $\frac{3}{8}$
    (D) $\frac{1}{2}$
    (E) $\frac{5}{8}$

6. Karen has $\frac{1}{3}$ of the peach pie and Mara has $\frac{1}{4}$ of the pie. Together, how much of the pie do they have?
    (A) $\frac{2}{12}$
    (B) $\frac{2}{4}$
    (C) $\frac{4}{3}$
    (D) $\frac{7}{12}$
    (E) $\frac{10}{12}$

Answer Key: Fractions

1. **Answer (D)** $\frac{27}{40}$

   $2 \times 20 = 40$ cards total. $\frac{27}{40}$ are "thank-you" cards.

2. **Answer (B)** $\frac{13}{40}$

   $40 - 27 = 13$. $\frac{13}{40}$ are "all occasion" cards.

3. **Answer (E)** $\frac{3}{5}$

   Five equal parts of which 3 are shaded = $\frac{3}{5}$

4. **Answer (C)** $\frac{4}{6}$

   Six equal parts of which 4 are shaded = $\frac{4}{6}$

5. **Answer (C)** $\frac{3}{8}$

   Eight equal parts of which 3 are shaded = $\frac{3}{8}$

6. **Answer (D)** $\frac{7}{12}$

   The lowest common denominator is 12 ($3 \times 4 = 12$).

   $\frac{1}{3} = \frac{4}{12}$

   $\frac{1}{4} = \frac{3}{12}$

   $\frac{4}{12} + \frac{3}{12} = \frac{7}{12}$

Quick Questions: Decimals

Our system of writing numbers uses the ten digits: **0, 1, 2, 3, 4, 5, 6, 7, 8, 9.**

The word "decimal" comes from the Latin word for ten. Each whole number greater than 9 is represented by a sum. **For example, 538:**

$$500 = 5(100) \text{ or } 5(10 \times 10)$$
$$30 = 3(10)$$
$$\underline{8} = 8(1)$$
$$538 = 5(100) + 30(10) + 8(1)$$

1. Write the decimal: two thousand five hundred sixty-three ten-thousandths.
   (A) 0.002563
   (B) 0.02563
   (C) 0.2563
   (D) 2.563
   (E) 2500.63

2. Choose the greatest of the numbers below:
   (A) 1.065
   (B) 1.654
   (C) 1.645
   (D) 1.456
   (E) 1.045

3. Eighty three one-hundredths of the 600 pencils in a box have no points. How many pencils have no points?
   (A) 83
   (B) 102
   (C) 138
   (D) 183
   (E) 498

Answer Key: Decimals

1. **Answer (C) 0.2563**

2. **Answer (B) 1.654**

3. **Answer (E) 498**
   $0.83 \times 600 = 498$

Quick Questions: Ratios

A ratio compares one quantity with another. When two numbers are compared by division, the indicated division is called a ratio. When two ratios are equal, these two ratios form a proportion. A ratio can be expressed in several ways. For example, the ratio 5 to 10 can be expressed as:

$$\frac{5}{10} \qquad 5 \div 10 \qquad 5{:}10$$

1. There are 12 boys and 8 girls in the Art Club. What is the ratio of boys to girls?
    (A) 1:20
    (B) 8:12
    (C) 8:20
    (D) 3:2
    (E) 20:1

2. A school reports a student to teacher ratio of 6:1. If there are 45 teachers in the school, how many students are there?
    (A) 51
    (B) 151
    (C) 225
    (D) 270
    (E) 285

3. The proportion of milk to coffee in Joe's famous "Café con Leche" is 6 to 5. In a 22-ounce mug, how many ounces are coffee?
    (A) 5
    (B) 6
    (C) 10
    (D) 12
    (E) 16

Answer Key: Ratios

1. **Answer (D) 3:2**
    12:8 = 3:2

2. **Answer (D) 270**
    Students ÷ teachers = $\frac{6}{1}$ = 6
    45 teachers × 6 = 270

3. **Answer (C) 10**
    6 parts milk to 5 parts coffee.
    6 parts + 5 parts = 11 parts.
    22 ounces ÷ 11 parts = 2 ounces per part.
    5 parts × 2 ounces/part = 10 ounces.

Quick Questions: Ordering of Numbers

The symbol > means "greater than." For example, 6 > 4 can be read as "six is greater than four."
The symbol < means "less than." $6x < 20$ can be read "six times some number is less than twenty."

1. Which of the following values of Δ makes this statement true?
   $-3 < \Delta < 2$

   (A) 5
   (B) 4
   (C) 3
   (D) –4
   (E) –1

2. If A > B and B > C and D > A, which is the correct order from largest to smallest?

   (A) D > A > B > C
   (B) D > A > C > B
   (C) A > C > B > D
   (D) D > C > B > A
   (E) B > C > A > D

Answer Key: Ordering of Numbers

1. **Answer (E) –1**
   $-3 < \Delta < 2$

2. **Answer (A) D > A > B > C**

Quick Questions: Positive and Negative Numbers

The whole numbers (0, 1, 2, 3...), together with their opposites (0, -1, -2, -3...), are called integers. The counting numbers (1, 2, 3...) are positive integers and are sometimes represented by the symbols +1, +2, +3... The numbers -1, -2, -3... are negative integers. The number 0 is neither positive nor negative. When two negative numbers are multiplied, the result is a positive integer.

1. An elevator is on the ground floor. It goes up 8 floors, then down 5 floors, and then up 4 floors. What is the final position in terms of the ground floor?
    (A) 3rd floor
    (B) 4th floor
    (C) 5th floor
    (D) 7th floor
    (E) 8th floor

2. One week the price of a shirt changed as follows: Monday, up $1; Tuesday, unchanged; Wednesday, down $2; Thursday, down $1; Friday, up $1. What is the net change in price?
    (A) $0
    (B) +$1
    (C) -$1
    (D) +$2
    (E) -$2

3. 8 × -4 × -3 =
    (A) -32
    (B) -27
    (C) 27
    (D) 32
    (E) 96

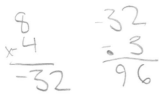

Answer Key: Positive and Negative Numbers

1. **Answer (D) 7th floor**
    8 +(−5) + 4 = 3 + 4 = 7

2. **Answer (C) −1**
    1 + 0 + (−2) + (−1) + 1 = 2 − 3 = −1

3. **Answer (E) 96**
    8 × −4 = −32; −32 × − 3 = 96

Quick Questions: Even & Odd Numbers

Even numbers are numbers that are divisible by the number two (2); when divided by two, the result is a whole number. **Odd numbers** are those numbers that are not divisible by the number two (2); when divided by two, the result includes a fraction. For example, 6 is an <u>even</u> number because $6 \div 2 = 3$ (a whole number), but 9 is an <u>odd</u> number because $9 \div 2 = 4\frac{1}{2}$ (a fraction).

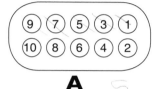

A

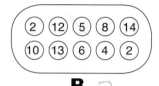

B

C

D

1. At a raffle, there are 4 jars that contain 10 balls each. In a drawing, which jar provides the LEAST chance for a person holding an odd-numbered raffle ticket to win?

   (A) A
   (B) B
   (C) C
   (D) D
   (E) They all have the same chance.

2. There are 56 children attending summer soccer camp. The camp director wants to organize the children into an even number of teams with an odd number of players on each team. If there must be the same number of children on each team, how many teams will there be?

   (A) 5
   (B) 6
   (C) 7
   (D) 8
   (E) 9

Answer Key: Even and Odd Numbers

1. **Answer (B) B**

2. **Answer (D) 8**

Quick Questions: Sequences

Sequences are number sets which follow a rule that places the numbers in a definite order. For example, "1, 3, 5, 7, 9" is a sequence that results from adding 2 to the first number to get the next number, then adding 2 to that number, and so on. Sequences can follow many patterns. The patterns are the result of the rule.

1. 2, 4, 8, 16, 32

   The rule for the sequence above is
   (A) square each number to produce the next number
   (B) add 2 to each number to produce the next number
   (C) divide each number by 2 to produce the next number
   (D) multiply each number by 2 to produce the next number
   (E) add the number before each number to the next number to produce the number after that

2. If the pattern of arrows shown in the figure continues to the right, in what direction will the 20th arrow point?
   (A) ↓
   (B) ↑
   (C) ↖
   (D) ↘
   (E) →

3. The figure shown depicts the top of a display of oranges at a market. How many oranges are in the next layer below those shown?
   (A) 10
   (B) 12
   (C) 13
   (D) 14
   (E) 15

   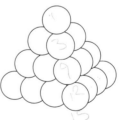

4. What is the next number in the following sequence? 0, 1, 1, 2, 3, 5, 8, 13, 21, __
   (A) 26
   (B) 30
   (C) 34
   (D) 42
   (E) 50

Answer Key: Sequences

1. **Answer (D)**

   $2 \times 2 = 4$; $4 \times 2 = 8$; $8 \times 2 = 16$; $16 \times 2 = 32$

   RULE: Multiply each number by 2 to produce the next number.

2. **Answer (E)** $\longrightarrow$

   Straight to the right $\longrightarrow$

3. **Answer (E) 15**

   Each layer has 3 sides. The top layer has 1 orange, the second layer has 3 oranges, the third layer has 6 oranges, and the fourth layer has 10 oranges (1 orange in the middle and 9 in the perimeter). The next layer will have 15 oranges (3 oranges in the middle and 12 in the perimeter).

4. **Answer (C) 34**

   Each number in the sequence is the sum of the two numbers preceding it in the sequence. $21 + 13 = 34$

Quick Questions: Frequency

When items in a group share at least one characteristic or attribute, the total number of those similar items is called their **frequency**. For example, the face of a clock has a dot at five-minute intervals. The frequency of those dots is <u>twelve</u> per clock ($60 \div 5 = 12$).

1. The numbers in the circle can be classified by the number of digits in the number. What is the frequency of the three-digit number group?

    (A) 3
    (B) 4
    (C) 5
    (D) 6
    (E) 7

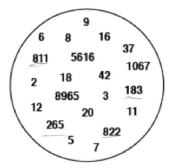

2. The names of the 15 children in the fifth grade at King School are listed below. How many letters are in the <u>second</u> most frequent length of name?

Robert 6	Annie 5	Marion 6	Albert 6	Thatcher 8
Emilio 6	Angela	Malcolm 7	Beth 4	Anthony 7
Tara 4	Shana 5	Ben 3	Bernadette 10	Chris 5

    (A) 3
    (B) 4
    (C) 5
    (D) 6
    (E) 7

    6:5   7:2   4:2
    5:3   8:1   3:1
                10:1

3. If buses arrive at a terminal with a frequency of one every two minutes, what is the frequency of arrivals every hour?

    (A) 10
    (B) 15
    (C) 20
    (D) 25
    (E) 30

    1 = 2 min   30 - 60 min   2)60‾ 30

Answer Key: Frequency

1. **Answer (B) 4**

2. **Answer (C) 5**

3. **Answer (E) 30**
    1 hour = 60 minutes. $60 \div 2 = 30$ arrivals per hour

Quick Questions: Algebra

Algebra uses numbers, symbols, and letter symbols to solve problems. The basic concept is that one side of the equal sign "=" is, in total, the same as the other. Another important item is the symbol ( ) which indicates that you make the calculations within the symbol (parentheses) before you make those outside the symbol.

In algebra, a letter is used to represent an unknown number until the value of that number is discovered. For example, when 5 is added to some unknown number, the sum is 14 and may be written as follows:

$$5 + n = 14$$

1. Molly has x dollars and Alex has 5 dollars more than Molly. If Alex gives Molly 6 dollars, how many dollars will Alex have left?

   (A) $x - 1$
   (B) $x + 1$
   (C) $5x + 1$
   (D) $6x + 1$
   (E) $6x - 1$

   $M = x$
   $A = x + 5 - 6 = -1$

2. Solve for x: $15(6 + 3) = x$

   (A) 24
   (B) 45
   (C) 90
   (D) 135
   (E) 150

   $15(6+3)$ $\frac{4|5}{.9}$
   $15 \cdot 9$ 135
   135

3. Calculate $2x - y^2$ when $x = 5$ and $y = 3$.

   (A) 1
   (B) 4
   (C) 0
   (D) 6
   (E) 15

   $2 \cdot 5 - 3^2$
   $2 \cdot 5 - 9$
   $10 - 9$

Answer Key: Algebra

1. **Answer (A) $x - 1$**
   $x + 5 - 6 = x - 1$

2. **Answer (D) 135**
   Simplify the multiplication on the left side of the = sign: $6 + 3 = 9$
   $15 \times 9 = x$
   $135 = x$

3. **Answer (A) 1**
   $2x - y^2 = $__ when $x = 5$ and $y = 3$; $2(5) - 3^2 = 10 - 9 = 1$

Quick Questions: Geometry and Measurement

> **Perimeter** refers to the distance around the outer boundary of a figure. **Area** refers to the measure of a surface. **Volume** refers to the three-dimensional measure of a shape.
>
> For example, the perimeter of this square is 5 + 5 + 5 + 5 = 20 units.
>
> The area is 5 × 5 = 25 square units.

1. Find the perimeter of the figure:
   - (A) 12.2 cm
   - (B) 15.8 cm
   - (C) 18.3 cm
   - (D) 19.4 cm
   - (E) 21.9 cm

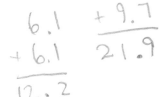

2. Find the perimeter of the figure:
   - (A) 8 units
   - (B) 10 units
   - (C) 16 units
   - (D) 32 units
   - (E) 64 units

3. Determine the area of the field:
   - (A) 500 sq ft
   - (B) 700 sq ft
   - (C) 15,000 sq ft
   - (D) 30,000 sq ft
   - (E) 37,000 sq ft

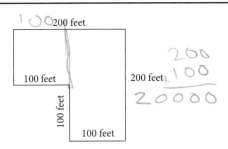

4. A case of <u>8 boxes</u> is packed as shown. If each box is a perfect cube measuring 5 inches to a side, what is the total volume of the case?
   - (A) 100 cubic inches
   - (B) 400 cubic inches
   - (C) 1000 cubic inches
   - (D) 2000 cubic inches
   - (E) 4000 cubic inches

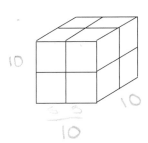

Answer Key: Geometry and Measurement

1. **Answer (E) 21.9 cm**

2. **Answer (B) 10 units**

3. **Answer (D) 30,000 sq ft**

   Convert the figure into two rectangles. One is 100 feet × 200 feet, and the other is 100 feet × 100 feet. Calculate the area by multiplying the length of the second side.

   100 × 200 = 20,000
   100 × 100 = 10,000
   20,000 + 10,000 = 30,000

4. **Answer (C) 1000 cubic inches**

Quick Questions: Angle Measurement

Angles are measured in **degrees**. Degrees are represented by the symbol °. For example, 45 degrees is expressed 45°. A circle contains 360°. The angles which make up a triangle equal 180°. A square or rectangle is made up of four 90° angles, for a total of 360°. The sum of angles which together form a straight line equals 180°.

1. When three lines meet as shown, what is the value of x?
    (A) 30°
    (B) 60°
    (C) 90°
    (D) 150°
    (E) 180°

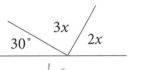

2. In the square shown, what is the value, in degrees, of x?
    (A) 45°
    (B) 90°
    (C) 125°
    (D) 135°
    (E) 180°

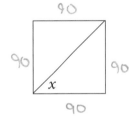

3. What is the value, in degrees, of the angle x enclosed by the circle?
    (A) 45°
    (B) 90°
    (C) 180°
    (D) 270°
    (E) 360°

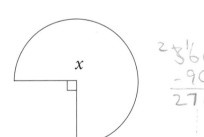

Answer Key: Angles

1. **Answer (A)** $x = 30°$
    $2x + 3x + 30° = 180°$
    $5x = 150°$

2. **Answer (A) 45°**

3. **Answer (D) 270°**
    The □ symbol indicates a 90° angle. A circle contains 360°.
    x = 360 – 90
    x = 270

Tri=180°
Quad=360°
Circle=360°

Quick Questions: Interpretation of Graphs

Graphs are used to present numerical information in visual form. A **bar graph** (A) is an easy way to compare quantities. A **line graph** (B) is used to record numerical changes over time. A **circle graph** (C) is used when a quantity is divisible into parts, and we want to compare the parts.

(A)   (B)   (C)

1. Approximately how much of his savings did John spend on a book?

   (A) $5
   (B) $10
   (C) $15
   (D) $20
   (E) $25

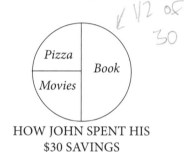

HOW JOHN SPENT HIS
$30 SAVINGS

2. If A represents 2 units and B represents 6 units, what does C represent?

   (A) 3 units
   (B) 4 units
   (C) 5 units
   (D) 7 units
   (E) 8 units

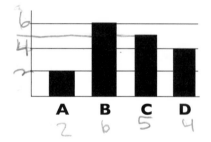

3. According to the graph, which segment represents the fastest segment of the trip?

   (A) AB
   (B) AC
   (C) BC
   (D) CD
   (E) DE

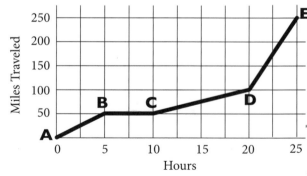

A Trip by Car

Answer Key: Interpretation of Graphs

1. **Answer (C) $15**

2. **Answer (C) 5 units**

3. **Answer (E) DE**

   Segment DE represents the greatest distance covered in the least amount of time.

3. The Reading Comprehension Section

By presenting passages and questions about the passages, the Reading Comprehension section measures your ability to understand what you read. After you read each passage, you'll be asked questions about its content or about the author's style, intent, or point of view. In general, the SSAT uses two types of writing: **narrative**, which includes excerpts from novels, poems, short stories, or essays; and **argument**, which presents a definite point of view about a subject. The passages are chosen from a variety of categories, including, but not limited to:

- **Humanities**: *art, biography, poetry, etc.*
- **Social Studies**: *history, economics, sociology, etc.*
- **Science**: *medicine, astronomy, zoology, etc.*

JUST THE FACTS

Reading Comprehension

Number of questions:
40

What it measures:
The questions measure your ability to read and comprehend what you read.

Scored section:
Yes.

Time allotted:
40 minutes

What are the Directions for the Reading Comprehension Section on the Test?

Read each passage carefully and then answer the questions about it. For each question, decide on the basis of the passage which one of the choices best answers the question.

What Types of Questions are Presented in the Reading Comprehension Section?

Most of the questions in the reading comprehension section focus on the following:

1. **Determining the main idea**

   Selecting the main idea in the passage
   Examples:
   - Which of the following best states the main idea of the passage?
   - The passage is primarily about…

   Choosing the best title for the passage
   Examples:
   - Which of the following is the best title for the selection?
   - The headline that best fits the article is…

2. Locating details

Understanding specific references or a section in the passage

Examples:

- According to the passage, what happens when the bell rings?
- In the first paragraph, the writer describes...

Identifying specific things about the passage

- The "beginning" (line 15) probably refers to...
- According to the author, who was Nelly visiting?

Determining key terms used in the passage

- As used in the sentence, "justification" (line 5) most nearly means...
- In line 13, the word "relinquish" means...

3. Drawing inferences

Fitting together ideas in the passage to determine their relationships

Examples:

- In the poem, the "rain," "sand," and "heat" (lines 1-3) suggest that...
- It can be inferred from the passage that the location of the event is most likely...

Assuming things about the passage even though they may not be stated directly

Examples:

- The water disappeared most likely because...
- "The rock is transformed" (line 25) probably means...

4. Identifying tone or mood

Determining the tone, mood, or style of the passage

Examples:

- The critic's tone can best be described as which of the following?
- The writer's style is best described as...

How are the Reading Comprehension Questions Presented?

The SSAT presents each passage (or poem) with a corresponding group of three to six questions for each passage. The directions instruct you to read each passage and answer the questions about it.

> Little Jim was, for the time, Engine Number 36 and he was making the run between Syracuse and Rochester. He was fourteen minutes behind time, and the throttle was wide open. As a result, when he swung around the curve at the flower bed, a wheel of his cart destroyed a tulip. Number 36 slowed down at once and looked guiltily at his father, who was mowing the lawn. The doctor had his back to the accident,
>
> Line 5 and he continued to pace slowly to and fro, pushing the mower.
>
> Jim dropped the handle of the cart. He looked at his father and at the broken flower. Finally, he went to the tulip and tried to stand it up, but it would only hang limply from his hand. Jim could not repair it. He looked again toward his father.

1. At the beginning of the passage, Jim was pretending that he was
   (A) driving a tractor
   (B) piloting an airplane
   (C) a passenger on a train
   (D) a speeding railroad engine
   (E) running a race with a freight train
   The correct answer is (D), a speeding railroad engine, as shown by the sentence, "Little Jim was, for the time, Engine Number 36."

2. According to the passage, Jim's father was a
   (A) farmer
   (B) doctor
   (C) gardener
   (D) train engineer
   (E) business executive
   The correct answer is (B), doctor. The passage states that after Jim destroyed the tulip, he looked at his father, who was mowing the lawn. The "doctor" (line 4) had his back to the accident.

3. Jim apparently thought that when his father saw the broken flower his reaction would be one of
   (A) fear
   (B) anger
   (C) curiosity
   (D) amusement
   (E) indifference
   The correct answer is (B), anger. The passage implies that Jim thinks his father will be angry at him, as evidenced by the last paragraph—Jim tries to repair the tulip.

How Do You Answer the Reading Comprehension Questions?

As you read, figure out the main idea in the passage or poem. Identify the important details that move the narrative along or create a mood or tone. In an argument, identify the details that support the writer's opinion. The first sentence of each paragraph will give you a general sense of the topic. Identify the topic of each paragraph and underline key facts. Try to figure out the writer's intention, or purpose of the passage. Notice the writer's attitude, tone, and general style.

These habits can help you understand what you read, whether you are taking the Middle Level SSAT, preparing for a history test, or getting ready to write an essay for your English class.

Reading Comprehension Test-Taking Strategies

1. Take time to read and understand the first sentence of each paragraph. This will provide you with a general sense of the topic.

2. Scan the answer choices, since they are generally short and provide excellent clues. If an answer choice refers you to a specific line in the passage, underline that line for reference.

3. Read each passage carefully. Follow the author's reasoning. Notice attitude, tone, and general style.

4. Pay attention to words such as always, never, every, and none. They may play an important role in the answer.

5. Identify the topic of each paragraph, key facts, and the author's purpose for writing. Underline the key facts for quick reference.

6. Remember to read for the characteristics of the passage, not for information or to acquire an understanding of the topic.

7. Read all answer choices carefully before you choose. When you find an answer choice that fails to satisfy the requirements of the question and statement, cross it out.

Quick Questions: Reading Comprehension

Directions: Read each passage carefully and then answer the questions about it. For each question, decide on the basis of the passage which one of the choices best answers the question.

Over five thousand years ago, people living in Mesopotamia developed a form of writing to record and communicate different types of information. The earliest writing was based on pictograms. Pictograms were used to communicate basic information about crops and taxes. Around 3100 B.C. people began to record amounts of different crops. Barley was one of the most
Line 5 important crops in southern Mesopotamia, so the scribes made a symbol that looked like a stalk of barley. Scribes drew the sign on soft clay tablets using a pointed tool, probably made out of a reed.

Over hundreds of years, the barley sign changed shape when the scribes used a writing tool with a squared-off end instead of a point. The end of this tool was used to press wedge shapes
10 into clay tablets. It is at this point that the signs became what we call cuneiform. Not only the shape, but also the use of the sign had been changing. The barley sign could now be used in two ways. It could represent barley and a sound. The Sumerian word for barley was 'she'. So the barley sign was used to represent the sound 'she' in a word. Cuneiform was used by people throughout the ancient Near East to write several different languages.

---

1. From the passage, one can infer that pictograms

    (A) were easy to use
    (B) were written on paper
    (C) represented early literature
    (D) represented Mesopotamian gods
    (E) were drawings of common objects

2. Cuneiform was

    (A) a language
    (B) a writing implement
    (C) an early form of writing
    (D) used only by the Sumerians
    (E) the Sumerian word for barley

3. The passage shows that writing evolved over centuries. "Evolved" most likely means

    (A) was static
    (B) changed forms
    (C) was agricultural
    (D) became more difficult
    (E) remained in Mesopotamia

4. A scribe was

    (A) a god
    (B) an artist
    (C) a farmer
    (D) a record keeper
    (E) an expert at languages

5. According to the passage, writing in Mesopotamia started off as pictures and changed to

    (A) grain
    (B) words
    (C) letters
    (D) symbols
    (E) numbers

At the beginning of time, only gods and goddesses lived on earth. They had to do all the work to grow food to eat. It was difficult and they had to work hard. Each god and goddess had a job to do. Some dug and planted the crops in the fields, while others brought water to the fields in ditches. The sun god, Utu, shone above the fields. They were not happy having to work so hard.

Line 5 They had a meeting to talk about ways to make the work easier. They went to get advice from Enki, the god of the fresh waters and wisdom, who was asleep in his underwater house. Enki suggested that he make creatures who could serve them by working the land. Then the lives of the gods and goddesses would be much easier. The gods and goddesses thought that Enki's plan was brilliant. He collected clay from the bottom of the river where he lived and used it to make

10 people. He breathed life into the people, but limited how long they would breathe on the earth. Only the gods and goddesses might live forever. The humans were put to work in the fields. Because they served the gods and goddesses, they provided them with their food and drink. The humans took water from the rivers and gave it to the lifeless lands. They tilled the soil and planted crops. They worked hard and brought the land to life. The gods and goddesses were happy.

6. Enki was the god of

(A) the sun
(B) the Earth
(C) the ocean
(D) river beds
(E) fresh waters

7. The gods and goddesses enjoyed

(A) creating humans
(B) working the fields
(C) irrigating the fields
(D) being served by people
(E) seeing people living on earth

8. The land was brought to life by

(A) Utu
(B) clay
(C) Enki
(D) crops
(E) water

9. People were created from

(A) sun
(B) dirt
(C) clay
(D) crops
(E) water

10. From the passage, one might infer that Enki was also god of all of the following EXCEPT

(A) lakes
(B) farming
(C) creation
(D) the rivers
(E) the moon

Answer Key: Reading Comprehension

1. **(E)** The passage doesn't say anything about how easy pictograms were to use. The passage states that the symbols were written on soft clay tablets and nothing about paper. It also clearly says that the information recorded was about taxes and crops and there is no suggestion of literature or the gods.

2. **(C)** The passage states that it was used to write several different languages, so it was not a language. It says that the shapes were made with a squared off tool, and that it was used by people throughout the ancient Near East.

3. **(B)** The passage describes the changes that writing went through, so it was clearly not static. Writing was a form to record agricultural information. The passage does not mention the difficulty connected with writing and it says that writing was used throughout the Near East.

4. **(D)** There is no mention of gods, artists, or farmers (farming, but not farmers) in the passage. One might infer that a scribe was good at ONE language, i.e., the one he was using, but there is no reason to assume that he was good at more than that. The passage does say that scribes drew the signs on the clay that recorded the information.

5. **(D)** The writing was often about grain but it did not become grain. The writing used symbols to put together words but numbers and letters are not mentioned in the passage.

6. **(E)** Utu was the god of the sun. There is no mention in the passage of any other specific gods or their realms.

7. **(D)** The gods clearly did not enjoy working on or irrigating the fields. There is no mention of whether they enjoyed the act of creating people or seeing them living, but they were happy when the people worked hard.

8. **(E)** Utu was important because of the sun. People were created by Enki from clay. The crops were a necessary part of the land but the passage states that the water brought the land to life.

9. **(C)** The passage clearly states that people were created from clay. The sun is mentioned, as are crops and water, but not as the material of creation. Dirt is not mentioned.

10. **(E)** Rivers and lakes generally contain fresh waters, and Enki is the god of fresh waters. Water is essential to farming (as are the people he created) and he might be considered the god of creation as he was responsible for creating people.

4. The Verbal Section

The verbal section of the Middle Level SSAT asks you identify **synonyms** and to interpret **analogies**. The synonym questions test the strength of your vocabulary. The analogy questions measure your ability to relate ideas to each other logically.

Synonyms

Synonyms are words that have the *same* or nearly the same meaning as another word. For example, *fortunate* is a synonym for *lucky*, *tidy* is a synonym for *neat*, and *difficult* is a synonym for *hard*. Synonym questions on the SSAT ask you to choose a word that has a meaning similar to a given word.

What are the Directions for the Synonym Section on the Test?

Each of the following questions consists of one word followed by five words or phrases. You are to select the one word or phrase whose meaning is closest to the word in capital letters.

How are the Synonym Questions Presented?

The Middle Level SSAT presents vocabulary questions as a single word in capital letters and your task is to choose the word that is most similar in meaning to the word in capital letters.

EXAMPLE

1. PREMONITION:
   (A) opening
   (B) firmness
   (C) discovery
   (D) conspiracy
   (E) forewarning

   The correct answer is (E), forewarning.

EXAMPLE

2. TOLERATE:
   (A) avoid
   (B) accept
   (C) donate
   (D) confuse
   (E) perceive

   The correct answer is (B), accept.

EXAMPLE

3. GIMMICK:
   (A) halting stride
   (B) careless error
   (C) sticky surface
   (D) ingenious device
   (E) counterfeit money

   The correct answer is (D), ingenious device.

JUST THE FACTS

The Verbal Section

Number of questions:
60—30 synonyms and 30 analogies

What it measures:
Vocabulary, verbal reasoning, and ability to relate ideas logically

Scored section:
Yes.

Time allotted:
40 minutes

How Do You Answer Synonym Questions?

There is only one correct response, so make sure you read the question carefully. There are no context clues in the Middle Level SSAT vocabulary format. If the word tested is unfamiliar to you, you could use the process of elimination to choose the correct answer. In other words, eliminate or cross out any of the words that you know are not the correct answer. In this way, you can narrow down your choices.

How Can You Build Your Vocabulary?

The best way to prepare is to read as much as you can to build your vocabulary. If you encounter an unfamiliar word in your reading, make sure you look it up in a dictionary (either online or print). Keep track of the word and its meaning on an index card, notepad, or in your notes on your smartphone. Keeping track of new words or words that are unfamiliar to you will help you build a tremendous vocabulary.

Another way to prepare is to learn the meaning of the word parts that make up many English words. These word parts consist of **prefixes, suffixes,** and **roots**. If you encounter an unfamiliar word, you could take apart the word and think about the parts.

> The greater your vocabulary, the greater your chance of getting the correct answer.

Prefixes: 35 + 36 + 44 = 115

Prefix	Meaning	Example
a-, an-	not, without, opposite to	antonym
ab-	from	absent
ad-	to, toward	advance
ante	before	anteroom
anti-	against, opposite	antibacterial
auto-	self	autobiography
bi-	two	bicycle
circum-	around	circumference
de-	away from	depart
dia-	through, across	diagonal
dis-	away from, not	disappear, disloyal
en-	put in, into	enter
ex-	out of, former	exit, exasperation
extra-	outside of, beyond	extraordinary
hyper-	over, more	hyperactive
il-, ir	not, without	illuminate, irritate
in-, im-	into, not	insert, impossible
inter-	between	interact
intra-	within	intrastate
macro-	large	macroeconomics
mal	bad, wrong	malady, malpractice
micro-	small	microscope
mono-	one	monopoly, monotonous
multi-	many	multicolor
non-	without, not	nonsense
peri-	around	perimeter
post-	after	postscript
pre-, pro-	before, forward	preview, prologue
semi- (also hemi-)	half	semicircle, hemisphere
sub-	under	subway, submarine
syn-	same time	synonym
trans-	across	transport, transit
tri-	three	tricycle
un-	not	unknowing
uni-	one, together	unity

Suffixes 36

Suffix	Meaning	Example
-able	able to be	habitable
-acy	state or quality	privacy
-al	act or process of	theatrical
-an (-ian)	relating to, belonging to	American
-ance, -ence	state or quality of	brilliance
-ant	a person who	supplicant
-arian	a person who	librarian
-ate	have or be characterized by	desolate
-cide	act of killing	genocide
-cracy	rule, government, power	aristocracy
-dom	place or state of being	wisdom
-dox	belief	orthodox
-en	become	smarten
-er, -or	one who	lover
-ese	relating to a place	Japanese
-esque	in the style of/like	arabesque, grotesque
-fy /-ify	make, cause	beautify, certify
-ful	full of	graceful
-gam/gamy	marriage, union	monogamous
-gon/gonic	angle	decagon
-hood	state, condition, or quality	parenthood
-ile	relating to, capable of	domicile, juvenile
-ious, -ous	characterized by	contagious
-ish	having the quality of	devilish
-ism	doctrine, belief	socialism
-ist	one who	dramatist
-ity, -ty	quality of	ferocity
-ive	having the nature of	talkative
-ize	become	prioritize
-log(ue)	word, speech	analogy, dialogue
-ment	condition of	commitment
-ness	state of being	faithfulness
-phile	one who loves	Francophile
-phobia	abnormal fear of	agoraphobia
-ship	position held	scholarship
-sion, -tion	state of being	abbreviation

Word Roots 44   G = Greek   L = Latin

Root	Meaning	Examples
annu, enni (L)	year	anniversary, perennial
anthrop (G)	man	anthropomorphism
ast(er)(G)	star	astrology, asterisk
audi (L)	hear	audible, audience
auto (G)	self	autobiography
bene (L)	good	beneficial
bio (G)	life	biography, biology
chrono (G)	time	chronology
civ (L)	citizen	civilization, civilian
cred (L)	believe	credential, creed
dem(o) (G)	people	democracy
dict (L)	say	dictation, dictator
duc (L)	lead, make	conduct, deduct
gen (L)	give birth	genesis, generation
geo (G)	earth	geometry
graph (G)	write	dysgraphia, graphic
jur, jus (L)	law	jurisprudence, juror
log, logue (L)	thought	logical
luc (L)	light	lucid, translucent
man(u) (L)	hand	manual, manufacture
mand, mend (L)	order	command
min (L)	small	minimal
mis, mit (L)	send	missile, transmit
nov (L)	new	novel
omni (L)	all	omnivore
pan (G)	all	pan-American, panacea
patr (G) pater (L)	father	patriot
path (G)	feel	sympathy
phil (G)	love	philosophy, Philadelphia
phon (G)	sound	phonetic, telephone
photo (G)	light	photosynthesis
poli (G)	city	political, politician
port (L)	carry	deport, report
qui(t) (L)	quiet, rest	tranquility, quiet
scrib, script (L)	write	prescribe
sens, sent (L)	feel	sentiment
sol (L)	sun	solarium

Word Roots   G = Greek   L = Latin

Root	Meaning	Examples
tele (G)	far off	television
terr (L)	earth	terrestrial
tract (L)	drag, draw	detract, tractor
vac (L)	empty	evacuation
vid, vis (L)	see	invisible, videographer
vit (L)	life	vitality, vitamin
zo (G)	life	zoology

Quick Questions: Synonyms

Directions: Each of the following questions consists of a word followed by five words or phrases. You are to select the one word or phrase whose meaning is closest to the word in capital letters.

1. APLOMB:
   (A) cunning
   (B) concern
   (C) contortion
   (D) composure
   (E) commotion

2. BRANDISH:
   (A) hide
   (B) waver
   (C) flourish
   (D) emerge
   (E) materialize

3. LUMINOUS:
   (A) dull
   (B) terse
   (C) gloomy
   (D) glowing
   (E) obscure

4. VERSATILE:
   (A) vigilant
   (B) variable
   (C) constant
   (D) unsightly
   (E) vulnerable

5. WAFT:
   (A) jut
   (B) dive
   (C) drift
   (D) settle
   (E) hasten

6. SWAGGER:
   (A) skip
   (B) strut
   (C) sway
   (D) stroll
   (E) stagger

7. SCURRY:
   (A) rush
   (B) bluff
   (C) crawl
   (D) worry
   (E) meander

8. EGREGIOUS:
   (A) trivial
   (B) hidden
   (C) flagrant
   (D) fragrant
   (E) contagious

Answer Key: Synonyms

1. **(D) composure**
2. **(C) flourish**
3. **(D) glowing**
4. **(B) variable**
5. **(C) drift**
6. **(B) strut**
7. **(A) rush**
8. **(C) flagrant**

Verbal Analogies

Analogies are a comparison between two things that are usually seen as different from each other but have some similarities. They help us understand things by making connections and seeing relationships between them based on knowledge we already possess. These types of comparisons play an important role in improving problem-solving and decision-making skills, in perception and memory, in communication and reasoning skills, and in reading and building vocabulary. Analogies help students to process information actively, make important decisions, and improve understanding and long-term memory. Considering the relationships stimulates critical and creative thinking.

> The analogy portion of the SSAT asks you to identify the answer that best matches the relationship between two words.

What are the Directions for the Verbal Analogies Section on the Test?

The following questions ask you to find relationships between words. For each question, select the answer choice that best completes the meaning of the sentence.

What are the Things to Remember when Doing Analogies?

Parts of Speech

If the words in the first pair express a "noun/adjective" or "verb/noun" relationship, for example, the second pair should show the same relationship between parts of speech.

Word Order

If the first pair expresses a particular relationship, the second pair must express the same relationship in the same order.

Exactness

Sometimes two or more of the given choices would make fairly good sense in the blank. When this happens, choose the answer that most exactly suits the relationship between the words in the question.

How are Verbal Analogies Presented in the SSAT?

The SSAT analogy questions are written using only words.

Two-part stem—"A" is to "B" as ...

In this form, you will be presented with two words in the **stem** (the words presented in the question) and given the task to select the option that contains the pair of words with the same relationship as the pair of words "A" and "B".

> **EXAMPLE**
>
> 1. Grimace is to pain as
>   (A) nod is to agreement
>   (B) delete is to insertion
>   (C) frown is to cheer
>   (D) try is to failure
>   (E) gape is to caution
>
> The correct answer is (A), nod is to agreement.

Three-part stem—"A" is to "B" as "C" is to...

Some analogies supply three of the four necessary words. In this form, you will be presented with three words in the stem and your task is to find the relationship between the first two words and then choose a word that is related to the third word in the same way.

> **EXAMPLE**
>
> 1. Reprieve is to punishment as remission is to
>   (A) payment
>   (B) disease
>   (C) recognition
>   (D) pride
>   (E) relative
>
> The correct answer is (D), disease.

What are Verbal Analogy Relationships?

Some of the most common analogy relationships that you will find on the SSAT include the following:

- **Opposites or antonyms:** up is to down as short is to tall
- **Synonyms or words with identical or similar meetings:** big is to large as little is to small
- **Characteristic:** pillow is to soft as blanket is to warm
- **Part to whole:** trunk is to tree as stem is to flower
- **Uses:** broom is to sweep as pencil is to write
- **Users:** hammer is to carpenter as brush is to painter
- **Category:** robin is to bird as shark is to fish
- **Product to Producer:** poem is to poet as sculptor is to statue
- **Degree:** snow is to blizzard as rain is to hurricane
- **Homonyms:** four is to for as see is to sea

How Do You Solve Verbal Analogy Questions?

A great strategy for solving analogies is to use the "bridge sentence." Bridge sentences help you recognize quickly the pair of words that makes up the answer by "plugging in" the answer pair into the bridge sentence that you created from the stem. If your bridge sentence works with both the stem and the answer pair, you've answered the question correctly.

But first, you should try to determine the meaning of the initial pair of words in the stem. Then figure out how the first two words are related. Next, create a bridge sentence that expresses that relationship. We've provided a list of relationships on the previous page, but remember that the list does not include all of the relationships that you might find on the Middle Level SSAT. Try your sentence using each answer choice. As soon as you determine that an answer choice does not fit, eliminate it as a possible answer and go to the next choice. If you find that there is more than one answer, or that there is no answer, go back to see if a different relationship—a different bridge sentence—fits better.

> Be careful of the order of the words when you're determining the corresponding relationships.

Keep in mind that the relationships between the words in analogies can take many forms. They may be opposites, such as *up* and *down*. They may be actions, such as *hop* and *rabbit*. The analogy may even involve combinations of relationships. Think about the words *airplane* and *helicopter*: each is a vehicle, someone operates each one (a pilot), and each has a particular place in which it operates (the sky). So an analogy for *airplane is to helicopter* might be *automobile is to truck*, because both are vehicles that have drivers and both operate on roads. Another analogy is *yacht is to submarine*, because both are vehicles, both have people who operate them, and both operate in water.

> If the analogy has a two-part stem, then review the pair of words in each answer choice and establish the relationship between the pair of words in the stem. If the analogy has a three-part stem, then review the answer choices and try to establish the relationship with the third word in the stem.

Try thinking of the analogy portion of the SSAT as the brainteaser section. When you're teasing out the meanings of analogies, don't focus only on the meanings of words. The relationship between the words is as important as their meanings. And the good news about analogies is that you can get better at solving them with practice!

The following analogy examples will give you an idea of how the SSAT analogy questions are presented. Each question corresponds to one of the "relationships" already discussed. Next, you'll get an opportunity to practice in the Quick Questions section that follows.

EXAMPLE

1. Ignite is to kindle as
   (A) falter is to run
   (B) jog is to sprint
   (C) narrate is to tell
   (D) speak is to shout
   (E) banish is to invite

The relationship above is one of synonyms. Both ignite and kindle mean "to set on fire" or "to make burn." To complete this analogy you must find the set of words in the options that are also synonyms. Answer choice (C) "narrate is to tell" is correct as narrate means "tell." Answer choices (A) and (E) are incorrect because the sets of words are opposites. Answer choices (B) and (D) are incorrect because the relationship between those words is that of degree. (Sprint is faster than jog and shout is louder than speak.)

EXAMPLE

2. Recluse is to sociable as jargon is to
   (A) deft
   (B) pristine
   (C) ominous
   (D) common
   (E) impending

The relationship above is one of opposites. A "recluse" is by definition NOT sociable. To complete this analogy, you must find the word is that is opposite of "jargon." Answer choice (D) "common" is correct because "jargon" is specialized language and therefore is NOT common. Answer choice (A) is incorrect because "deft" means "skillful." Answer choice (B) is incorrect because "pristine" means "unspoiled." Answer choice (C) is incorrect because "ominous" means "threatening." Answer choice (E) is incorrect because "impending" means "approaching." None of these words has anything to do with jargon.

Verbal Test-Taking Strategies

1. The best way to improve your vocabulary is to read, read, and read some more.

2. Take note of unfamiliar words and look up their meanings.

3. Review the words you don't know.

4. Practice your vocabulary by taking the practice tests in this book. If you missed any of the verbal questions, read the questions and answers again, so you'll understand why you answered those questions incorrectly. Look them up and write them down.

5. Read as much as you can!

Quick Questions: Analogies

Directions: The following questions ask you to find relationships between words. For each question, select the answer choice that best completes the meaning of the sentence.

1. Circumference is to perimeter as
    (A) arc is circle
    (B) sum is to total
    (C) pie is to graph
    (D) product is to multiply
    (E) numerator is to denominator

2. Ember is to ignite as
    (A) dry is towel
    (B) bark is to dog
    (C) hammer is to tool
    (D) water is to douse
    (E) cover is to blanket

3. Knoll is to mountain as stream is to
    (A) tree
    (B) lake
    (C) river
    (D) valley
    (E) ocean

4. Translucent is to opaque as light is to
    (A) sun
    (B) dull
    (C) lamp
    (D) candle
    (E) darkness

5. Zeal is to kneel as
    (A) up is to down
    (B) quell is to spell
    (C) your is to their
    (D) apathy is to standing
    (E) gusto is to enthusiasm

6. Jabber is to blabber is
    (A) talk is sing
    (B) run is to jump
    (C) whirl is to twirl
    (D) read is to recite
    (E) lecture is to teach

Answer Key: Analogies

1. **(B) sum is to total**
    The relationship is one of synonyms. Circumference is the boundary line of a figure just as perimeter is and a sum is a total. An arc is part of a circle. A pie chart is a kind of graph. The product is the answer to a multiplication problem. The numerator is the number on the top of a fraction and the denominator is the number at the bottom. None of those are synonyms.

2. **(D) water is to douse**
    The relationship is one of item to its use. An ember can be used to ignite a flame and water can be used to douse a flame. Dry is what a towel is used for (backwards relationship) as a blanket can be used to cover someone/thing. Dogs bark and a hammer is a kind of tool.

3. **(C) river**
    The relationship is one of degree. A knoll is a mound or small hill and a mountain is a large mound. A stream is a small body of running water and a river is a large one. Tree, lake, valley and ocean are all natural occurrences, but are not connected by degree to stream.

4. **(E) darkness**
    The relationship is of opposites. Something translucent allows light through, and something opaque does not. Sun makes things light, as do a lamp and a candle. Dull is not connected to light.

5. **(B) quell is to spell**
    The relationship is of rhymes. The words rhyme as do zeal and kneel. None of the other word pairs rhyme. Up and down are opposites. Your and there are possessives. Apathy and standing have no real connection and gusto and enthusiasm are synonyms.

6. **(C) whirl is to twirl**
    The relationship is of rhyming synonyms. The words rhyme and mean nearly the same thing as do jabber and blabber. Talk and sing are both vocal activities. Run and jump are fun activities. One must read in order to recite and sometimes people teach by lecturing.

Summing It Up

Here are a few things to keep in mind when you take the Middle Level SSAT:

- Make sure that you understand the directions before you start to work on any section. If there is anything that you do not understand, read the directions again.

- You don't need to answer every question on the test to score well. Some of the questions will be very easy and others will be difficult. Whenever the test is administered, most students find that they do not know the answer to every question in every section. By working as quickly as you can without rushing, you should be able to read and think about every question.

- If you are not sure of an answer to a question, put a question mark (?) in the margin and move on. Make sure you also skip that question's answer bubble on your answer sheet! If you have time, you can come back to questions you have not answered.

- You may make as many marks on the test booklet as you need to. Just be sure to mark your answers on the answer sheet!

- Answers written in the test book will not count toward your score. Space is provided in the book for scratch work in the quantitative sections. Check often to make sure that you are marking your answer in the correct row on the answer sheet.

- If you decide to change an answer, be sure to erase your first mark on the answer sheet completely.

Chapter Three: Scores

What Your Scores Mean

If you're like most people, you'll quickly scan the score report trying to find <u>the</u> **magic** number that will tell you whether the scores are good or bad. With an admission test like the SSAT, this is not an easy thing to do. First, one must remember that the purpose of an admission test is to offer a common measure of academic ability, which can be used to compare all applicants. In the case of the SSAT, the test-taker population is a relatively homogenous one—students applying to college-preparatory private/independent schools. Given this, it is important to keep in mind that the test taker's scores are being compared only to students in this academically elite group.

> Most people are not aware that a "good" admission test question is only answered correctly fifty percent of the time.

As described in Chapter 1, admission tests differ from other tests such as classroom and achievement tests in significant ways. Achievement and classroom tests both assess a specific body of knowledge that should have been covered in the class and school year. If all students perform well, the teacher and school system have fulfilled their objective. If all students performed well on an admission test, it would lose its value in helping differentiate between and among candidates. Most people are not aware that a "good" admission test question is only answered correctly fifty percent of the time. The overall difficulty level of the SSAT is built to be at fifty percent. Thus, it's fair to say that the SSAT is difficult because *it is supposed to be.*

Formula Scoring

The SSAT uses a method of scoring known in the testing industry as "Formula Scoring." The SSAT was originally developed by ETS in the 1950s, and the model was very much that of a junior SAT, which also utilizes formula scoring. Students earn one point for every correct answer, no points for omitted questions, and lose ¼ point for each incorrect answer.

Test takers are instructed to omit questions for which they cannot make an educated guess. Since most students have not encountered this kind of a test before, it is an important area for students to understand and to have some experience in prior to taking the SSAT. SSAT score reports provide detailed information by section on the number of questions right, wrong, and omitted to aid families and schools in understanding the student's test-taking strategy and scores.

What do Admission Officers Consider?

It cannot be said often enough: *admission test scores are only one piece of the application.* The degree of emphasis placed on scores in a school's admission process depends on that school and on other information, such as transcript and teacher recommendations.

Admission officers typically focus on the SSAT Scaled Score and the SSAT Percentile. They do <u>not</u> utilize the National Percentile (more on that later). The SSAT Scaled Score offers the most precise measure of a student's performance and is consistent over time (meaning a scaled score today means the same thing it did last year and 50 years ago). The SSAT Percentile is useful in comparing the student's performance to that of others *in this testing year*.

Ⓐ About You

Review this section carefully. Is the student's name spelled correctly? Is the date of birth listed correctly? And, very important, when registering the student did you list her/his *current* grade? The current grade is used to determine which test form the student will take and also dictates the comparison or norm group (SSAT Percentile). If you mistakenly listed the grade to which your child is applying instead, he/she may get the wrong form and his/her SSAT Scaled Score will be compared with students a year (or grade) older. If any of this information is incorrect, contact SSATB immediately.

Ⓑ The Test You Took

Again, review this information for accuracy. For Test Level, the student will have taken either the Middle Level SSAT for students in grades 5-7, who are applying to grades 6-8, or the Upper Level SSAT for students in grades 8-11, who are applying to grades 9-12. There is a different score scale for each of these levels.

Ⓒ SSAT Score

SSAT scores are broken down by section, so you can understand the student's performance on each of the three scored sections (Verbal, Quantitative/Math, Reading). A total score (a sum of the three sections) is also reported.

For the Middle Level SSAT the lowest number on the scale (440) is the lowest possible score a student can earn and the highest number (710) the highest score. The SSAT is scored on a bell curve, thus 50% of students score above the mean (or average) and 50% below. In trying to understand the student's SSAT Score, it may be helpful first to consider if it is at, above, or below the Mean.

Ⓓ Personal Score Range

The student's SSAT score falls right in the middle of their "Personal Score Range". As a statistically valid and reliable standardized admission test, the SSAT has undergone extensive studies. Results of these studies indicate that should a student take another version of the SSAT within a short period of time their scores will fall within one Standard Error of Measurement (SEM) of their previous score. For the Middle Level SSAT, the SEM is 18 points. A score that falls within one SEM of a previous score is not statistically different.

Continued on Page 60

Secondary School Admission Test Score Report

About You

Name
SSAT SAMPLE

Grade
5

Sex
Female

Date of Birth
01 Jan 2002

SSAT SAMPLE
1234 SECOND STREET
SUBURB, NJ 01234

The Test You Took B

Registration ID
300000000

Test Date
01 Aug 2012

Test Level
Middle

Test Center
SSAT Sample
School (0000)

Your Scores

Middle Level Score Range: 440-710

	SSAT Scaled Score	Personal Score Range	SSAT Percentile
Verbal	686	668 - 704	98
Math	623	608 - 638	78
Reading	683	665 - 701	98
Total	1,992		97

(C) (D) (E)

What Does My Score Mean, and Why Do I Have a Personal Score Range?

Your scores are calculated by adding one point for each correct answer, zero points for each omitted question, and by subtracting one-quarter of one point for each incorrect answer or question with more than one answer marked. Independent schools vary in their approach to using test scores in the application process for admission. You are welcome to contact the schools of interest to you to learn how they use the SSAT. Since no standardized test score can exactly represent a student's ability in a particular area, we provide a personal score range. If a student takes different editions of the SSAT within a short period of time, it's likely that scores may vary but will nearly always fall within the student's personal score range.

What Does My SSAT Percentile Mean?

Your SSAT percentile is a score between 1 and 99. Your score compares your performance on the test to the performances of the other students of the same grade and gender who have taken the SSAT within the past three years. For example, if seventh-grader Sue Smith received a 65 SSAT percentile, she did as well as or better than 65% of the other 7th grade girls who took the SSAT in the past three years. If you are concerned that your percentiles are lower than you have earned on other tests, please remember that SSAT test takers are members of a small and highly competitive group of students who plan to attend some of the world's best independent schools. You should not be discouraged by what seems to be a lower score than you usually attain on standardized testing. Below is the average SSAT score received by a student of your grade and gender.

Average Grade	Verbal	Math	Reading
Grade 5 Female	590	589	592

Test Question Breakdown

		Right	Wrong	Omitted
Verbal Questions testing your knowledge of words (synonyms) and your ability to relate ideas (analogies).	Synonyms	22	6	2
	Analogies	24	3	3
Math Questions testing your knowledge of number properties and relationships, basic computation, elementary concepts of equivalencies, geometry, measurement, and interpretation of charts/graphs.	Number Concepts & Operations	15	7	2
	Algebra, Geometry & Other Math	16	9	1
Reading Questions regarding the main idea and supporting details of a passage or requiring higher order skills, such as deriving the meaning of words from context, extracting the meaning of a passage, or interpreting an author's logic, attitude and tone.	Main Idea	12	5	1
	Higher Order	17	4	1

Estimated National Percentile

Provided for students in grades 5-9 only.
The National Percentile, an estimated rank, compares your score to a hypothetical pool of all students in your grade level across the U.S. The national percentile rank is generally higher than the SSAT percentile rank, as test-takers are compared with a wide group of students from varying backgrounds, not just those who have taken the SSAT.

Estimated National Percentile	Verbal	Math	Reading
	98	98	98

Middle Level SSAT Score Scale = 440-710 (575 Mean, or average, score)

E SSAT Percentile

The SSAT Percentile is a score between 1 and 99. This number <u>compares</u> the student's performance on the SSAT with that of other students same grade/same gender, who have taken the SSAT in the previous three years. This "norm group" includes only those tests taken on one of the eight SSAT Standard test dates in the U.S. and Canada and, for students who have taken the SSAT more than once, only their first set of scores is included. So, on this sample report, the student's verbal score of 686, with a corresponding SSAT Percentile of 98, means that she scored as well or better than 98% of the 8th grade girls who took the SSAT in the U.S. and Canada over the previous three years on one of the eight SSAT Standard test dates.

Many parents express concern that their child's SSAT Percentile is lower than they typically score on other tests such as standardized achievement tests and school exams.

International and Flex Test scores are not included in the comparison group above. While they are not part of the norm group described above, their Scale Scores are compared to the domestic/Standard/first-time tester group described above.

> It is important to remember that SSAT test takers are members of a small and highly-competitive group of students who plan to attend some of the world's best private/independent schools. Being in the middle of this group is still impressive!

F Test Question Breakdown

This section provides useful and detailed information about the test's content and the student's test-taking strategies. Look carefully at the ratio of wrong answers to omits. If the student had many wrong answers, but omitted few or no questions, that would have an adverse effect on scores.

G Estimated National Percentile

The Estimated National Percentile is provided for students in grades 5-9. In most cases, the SSAT is the first time a family has seen their student compared to an academically elite group of college-bound students, and the scores may be "lower than normal." The Estimated National Percentile places the student's performance in the context of all students nationally, not just those applying to private/independent schools. Thus, the Estimated National Percentile is generally much higher than the SSAT Percentile. While this metric is included on score reports to provide this important context for families, it is not generally used by admission officers, who utilize the Scale Scores and SSAT percentile for the purpose of differentiating the performance of applicants.

Parent's Corner: Supporting Your Test Taker

Here are a few simple things you can do to help your student perform as well as possible on the Middle Level SSAT without creating too much anxiety.

Practice! Practice! Practice! Help your student structure practice time to take the Middle Level SSAT Practice Tests in the next chapter. Act as the proctor—administer the timed practice tests, while approximating the standard testing conditions as closely as possible (no notes, no talking, no computer, no calculator).

Review and encourage! Review any incorrect answers that your student may have chosen. Which sections or types of questions proved most difficult for your student to answer? Focus, encourage, and help your student sharpen those skills. Try to figure out the cause of the errors so that your student can develop a strategy for avoiding similar mistakes on the actual test.

Some common pitfalls:
- Accidentally marking the wrong circle on the answer sheet even when the student knows the answer
- Making simple arithmetic mistakes

Double-checking answers and not rushing can (often) help with this.

Extra help! If taking the practice tests reveals that your student lacks a particular skill that is necessary for success, seeking extra help for your student may be useful.

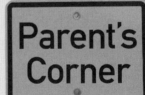

Perspective is everything! Keep the importance of the SSAT in perspective and help your student do the same. The SSAT is an important and valuable part of the application package and students should prepare for it. But remember that the SSAT is just *one* part of the entire package. Schools will weigh your student's test scores along with other information.

Retaking the test? Should your student want to retake the Middle Level SSAT, many options are available. But experience has shown that test scores rarely improve significantly when the test is retaken, unless there were extenuating circumstances that may have affected the student's performance, such as an illness or unusual emotional upset.

Rest up and eat well! Make sure your student gets enough sleep during the days leading up to the test, and eats a healthy breakfast on the day it is administered.

Be prepared for the unexpected! If your student panics, freezes, or gets sick during the administration of the SSAT, she or he has the option to leave the test. It's important for you to know that if your child does leave the test, the results will be cancelled. It's your responsibility, however, to alert SSATB immediately so that the scores are voided and not sent to schools. Please note that your fee for the cancelled test will not be refunded, but for a service charge, you may change to a new test date.

Middle Level
Practice Tests

Trying Out the Middle Level SSAT

Now it's time to find out what it's actually like to take the Middle Level SSAT. Ask a parent or other adult to help you set up a simulation—a re-creation of the experience that is as close as possible to what taking the Middle Level SSAT will be like. Think of it as a dress rehearsal for the real thing. Simulating the SSAT experience can help you walk into the testing center with more confidence and clarity about what to expect.

Remove (or photocopy) the answer sheet and use it to complete each practice test.

You can choose to do your simulation section by section or by taking an entire test from start to finish.

Here are the rules you'll need to follow to make your SSAT simulation as realistic as possible:

- Ask your "test proctor" to keep time and tell you when to begin and end each section.

- No talking or music is allowed during the SSAT, so make sure the room you are taking the test in is quiet, and turn off anything that makes noise, such as your phone, iPod, or TV.

- You will not be allowed to use any research material while taking the Middle Level SSAT, so put away your smartphone, laptop, books, dictionary, calculator, ruler, and notes.

- Work only on one section during the time allotted. Do not go back to another section to finish unanswered questions.

- Use sharpened #2 pencils and an eraser.

- Fill in the answer sheet (located before each test in the book) just as you would during a regular test.

Simulating the Test: Section by Section

If your goal is to sharpen your test-taking techniques in a specific area, use the individual sections for the simulation. Review the exercises in Chapter 2 before beginning, and be sure to follow the instructions for each section carefully. Schedule the allotted time for each section, and either ask the person supervising your simulation to time you or set a timer for yourself.

As you will when you actually take the Middle Level SSAT, mark your answer choices on the answer sheet.

Simulating the Test: Start to Finish

If your goal is to practice taking the entire Middle Level SSAT (minus the experimental section), here's how to schedule your time blocks, including breaks:

Test Overview		
Section	**Number of Questions**	**Time Allotted To Administer Each Section**
Writing Sample	1	25 minutes
Break		5 minutes
Section 1 (Quantitative)	25	30 minutes
Section 2 (Reading)	40	40 minutes
Break		10 minutes
Section 3 (Verbal)	60	30 minutes
Section 4 (Quantitative)	25	30 minutes
Totals	151	**2 hours, 50 minutes**

When you add this all up, you'll see that the total testing time is 2 hours and 35 minutes. When you add in the two breaks, the total time is 2 hours and 50 minutes (these practice tests do not include an experimental section). Be sure to use your breaks for stretching, getting a drink of water, and focusing your eyes on something other than a test paper. This will help clear your mind and get you ready for the next section.

A note about special timing: Students who have diagnosed learning differences may apply for and be granted special testing accommodations. Some students are granted "time and a half," and they are given 1.5 times the minutes available for each test section—including the writing sample and experimental section.

Practice Test I: Middle Level Answer Sheet

Be sure each mark completely fills the answer space.
Start with number 1 for each new section of the test. You may find more answer spaces than you need.
If so, please leave them blank.

Section 1

1 Ⓐ Ⓑ Ⓒ Ⓓ Ⓔ	6 Ⓐ Ⓑ Ⓒ Ⓓ Ⓔ	11 Ⓐ Ⓑ Ⓒ Ⓓ Ⓔ	16 Ⓐ Ⓑ Ⓒ Ⓓ Ⓔ	21 Ⓐ Ⓑ Ⓒ Ⓓ Ⓔ
2 Ⓐ Ⓑ Ⓒ Ⓓ Ⓔ	7 Ⓐ Ⓑ Ⓒ Ⓓ Ⓔ	12 Ⓐ Ⓑ Ⓒ Ⓓ Ⓔ	17 Ⓐ Ⓑ Ⓒ Ⓓ Ⓔ	22 Ⓐ Ⓑ Ⓒ Ⓓ Ⓔ
3 Ⓐ Ⓑ Ⓒ Ⓓ Ⓔ	8 Ⓐ Ⓑ Ⓒ Ⓓ Ⓔ	13 Ⓐ Ⓑ Ⓒ Ⓓ Ⓔ	18 Ⓐ Ⓑ Ⓒ Ⓓ Ⓔ	23 Ⓐ Ⓑ Ⓒ Ⓓ Ⓔ
4 Ⓐ Ⓑ Ⓒ Ⓓ Ⓔ	9 Ⓐ Ⓑ Ⓒ Ⓓ Ⓔ	14 Ⓐ Ⓑ Ⓒ Ⓓ Ⓔ	19 Ⓐ Ⓑ Ⓒ Ⓓ Ⓔ	24 Ⓐ Ⓑ Ⓒ Ⓓ Ⓔ
5 Ⓐ Ⓑ Ⓒ Ⓓ Ⓔ	10 Ⓐ Ⓑ Ⓒ Ⓓ Ⓔ	15 Ⓐ Ⓑ Ⓒ Ⓓ Ⓔ	20 Ⓐ Ⓑ Ⓒ Ⓓ Ⓔ	25 Ⓐ Ⓑ Ⓒ Ⓓ Ⓔ

Section 2

1 Ⓐ Ⓑ Ⓒ Ⓓ Ⓔ	9 Ⓐ Ⓑ Ⓒ Ⓓ Ⓔ	17 Ⓐ Ⓑ Ⓒ Ⓓ Ⓔ	25 Ⓐ Ⓑ Ⓒ Ⓓ Ⓔ	33 Ⓐ Ⓑ Ⓒ Ⓓ Ⓔ
2 Ⓐ Ⓑ Ⓒ Ⓓ Ⓔ	10 Ⓐ Ⓑ Ⓒ Ⓓ Ⓔ	18 Ⓐ Ⓑ Ⓒ Ⓓ Ⓔ	26 Ⓐ Ⓑ Ⓒ Ⓓ Ⓔ	34 Ⓐ Ⓑ Ⓒ Ⓓ Ⓔ
3 Ⓐ Ⓑ Ⓒ Ⓓ Ⓔ	11 Ⓐ Ⓑ Ⓒ Ⓓ Ⓔ	19 Ⓐ Ⓑ Ⓒ Ⓓ Ⓔ	27 Ⓐ Ⓑ Ⓒ Ⓓ Ⓔ	35 Ⓐ Ⓑ Ⓒ Ⓓ Ⓔ
4 Ⓐ Ⓑ Ⓒ Ⓓ Ⓔ	12 Ⓐ Ⓑ Ⓒ Ⓓ Ⓔ	20 Ⓐ Ⓑ Ⓒ Ⓓ Ⓔ	28 Ⓐ Ⓑ Ⓒ Ⓓ Ⓔ	36 Ⓐ Ⓑ Ⓒ Ⓓ Ⓔ
5 Ⓐ Ⓑ Ⓒ Ⓓ Ⓔ	13 Ⓐ Ⓑ Ⓒ Ⓓ Ⓔ	21 Ⓐ Ⓑ Ⓒ Ⓓ Ⓔ	29 Ⓐ Ⓑ Ⓒ Ⓓ Ⓔ	37 Ⓐ Ⓑ Ⓒ Ⓓ Ⓔ
6 Ⓐ Ⓑ Ⓒ Ⓓ Ⓔ	14 Ⓐ Ⓑ Ⓒ Ⓓ Ⓔ	22 Ⓐ Ⓑ Ⓒ Ⓓ Ⓔ	30 Ⓐ Ⓑ Ⓒ Ⓓ Ⓔ	38 Ⓐ Ⓑ Ⓒ Ⓓ Ⓔ
7 Ⓐ Ⓑ Ⓒ Ⓓ Ⓔ	15 Ⓐ Ⓑ Ⓒ Ⓓ Ⓔ	23 Ⓐ Ⓑ Ⓒ Ⓓ Ⓔ	31 Ⓐ Ⓑ Ⓒ Ⓓ Ⓔ	39 Ⓐ Ⓑ Ⓒ Ⓓ Ⓔ
8 Ⓐ Ⓑ Ⓒ Ⓓ Ⓔ	16 Ⓐ Ⓑ Ⓒ Ⓓ Ⓔ	24 Ⓐ Ⓑ Ⓒ Ⓓ Ⓔ	32 Ⓐ Ⓑ Ⓒ Ⓓ Ⓔ	40 Ⓐ Ⓑ Ⓒ Ⓓ Ⓔ

Section 3

1 Ⓐ Ⓑ Ⓒ Ⓓ Ⓔ	13 Ⓐ Ⓑ Ⓒ Ⓓ Ⓔ	25 Ⓐ Ⓑ Ⓒ Ⓓ Ⓔ	37 Ⓐ Ⓑ Ⓒ Ⓓ Ⓔ	49 Ⓐ Ⓑ Ⓒ Ⓓ Ⓔ
2 Ⓐ Ⓑ Ⓒ Ⓓ Ⓔ	14 Ⓐ Ⓑ Ⓒ Ⓓ Ⓔ	26 Ⓐ Ⓑ Ⓒ Ⓓ Ⓔ	38 Ⓐ Ⓑ Ⓒ Ⓓ Ⓔ	50 Ⓐ Ⓑ Ⓒ Ⓓ Ⓔ
3 Ⓐ Ⓑ Ⓒ Ⓓ Ⓔ	15 Ⓐ Ⓑ Ⓒ Ⓓ Ⓔ	27 Ⓐ Ⓑ Ⓒ Ⓓ Ⓔ	39 Ⓐ Ⓑ Ⓒ Ⓓ Ⓔ	51 Ⓐ Ⓑ Ⓒ Ⓓ Ⓔ
4 Ⓐ Ⓑ Ⓒ Ⓓ Ⓔ	16 Ⓐ Ⓑ Ⓒ Ⓓ Ⓔ	28 Ⓐ Ⓑ Ⓒ Ⓓ Ⓔ	40 Ⓐ Ⓑ Ⓒ Ⓓ Ⓔ	52 Ⓐ Ⓑ Ⓒ Ⓓ Ⓔ
5 Ⓐ Ⓑ Ⓒ Ⓓ Ⓔ	17 Ⓐ Ⓑ Ⓒ Ⓓ Ⓔ	29 Ⓐ Ⓑ Ⓒ Ⓓ Ⓔ	41 Ⓐ Ⓑ Ⓒ Ⓓ Ⓔ	53 Ⓐ Ⓑ Ⓒ Ⓓ Ⓔ
6 Ⓐ Ⓑ Ⓒ Ⓓ Ⓔ	18 Ⓐ Ⓑ Ⓒ Ⓓ Ⓔ	30 Ⓐ Ⓑ Ⓒ Ⓓ Ⓔ	42 Ⓐ Ⓑ Ⓒ Ⓓ Ⓔ	54 Ⓐ Ⓑ Ⓒ Ⓓ Ⓔ
7 Ⓐ Ⓑ Ⓒ Ⓓ Ⓔ	19 Ⓐ Ⓑ Ⓒ Ⓓ Ⓔ	31 Ⓐ Ⓑ Ⓒ Ⓓ Ⓔ	43 Ⓐ Ⓑ Ⓒ Ⓓ Ⓔ	55 Ⓐ Ⓑ Ⓒ Ⓓ Ⓔ
8 Ⓐ Ⓑ Ⓒ Ⓓ Ⓔ	20 Ⓐ Ⓑ Ⓒ Ⓓ Ⓔ	32 Ⓐ Ⓑ Ⓒ Ⓓ Ⓔ	44 Ⓐ Ⓑ Ⓒ Ⓓ Ⓔ	56 Ⓐ Ⓑ Ⓒ Ⓓ Ⓔ
9 Ⓐ Ⓑ Ⓒ Ⓓ Ⓔ	21 Ⓐ Ⓑ Ⓒ Ⓓ Ⓔ	33 Ⓐ Ⓑ Ⓒ Ⓓ Ⓔ	45 Ⓐ Ⓑ Ⓒ Ⓓ Ⓔ	57 Ⓐ Ⓑ Ⓒ Ⓓ Ⓔ
10 Ⓐ Ⓑ Ⓒ Ⓓ Ⓔ	22 Ⓐ Ⓑ Ⓒ Ⓓ Ⓔ	34 Ⓐ Ⓑ Ⓒ Ⓓ Ⓔ	46 Ⓐ Ⓑ Ⓒ Ⓓ Ⓔ	58 Ⓐ Ⓑ Ⓒ Ⓓ Ⓔ
11 Ⓐ Ⓑ Ⓒ Ⓓ Ⓔ	23 Ⓐ Ⓑ Ⓒ Ⓓ Ⓔ	35 Ⓐ Ⓑ Ⓒ Ⓓ Ⓔ	47 Ⓐ Ⓑ Ⓒ Ⓓ Ⓔ	59 Ⓐ Ⓑ Ⓒ Ⓓ Ⓔ
12 Ⓐ Ⓑ Ⓒ Ⓓ Ⓔ	24 Ⓐ Ⓑ Ⓒ Ⓓ Ⓔ	36 Ⓐ Ⓑ Ⓒ Ⓓ Ⓔ	48 Ⓐ Ⓑ Ⓒ Ⓓ Ⓔ	60 Ⓐ Ⓑ Ⓒ Ⓓ Ⓔ

Section 4

1 Ⓐ Ⓑ Ⓒ Ⓓ Ⓔ	6 Ⓐ Ⓑ Ⓒ Ⓓ Ⓔ	11 Ⓐ Ⓑ Ⓒ Ⓓ Ⓔ	16 Ⓐ Ⓑ Ⓒ Ⓓ Ⓔ	21 Ⓐ Ⓑ Ⓒ Ⓓ Ⓔ
2 Ⓐ Ⓑ Ⓒ Ⓓ Ⓔ	7 Ⓐ Ⓑ Ⓒ Ⓓ Ⓔ	12 Ⓐ Ⓑ Ⓒ Ⓓ Ⓔ	17 Ⓐ Ⓑ Ⓒ Ⓓ Ⓔ	22 Ⓐ Ⓑ Ⓒ Ⓓ Ⓔ
3 Ⓐ Ⓑ Ⓒ Ⓓ Ⓔ	8 Ⓐ Ⓑ Ⓒ Ⓓ Ⓔ	13 Ⓐ Ⓑ Ⓒ Ⓓ Ⓔ	18 Ⓐ Ⓑ Ⓒ Ⓓ Ⓔ	23 Ⓐ Ⓑ Ⓒ Ⓓ Ⓔ
4 Ⓐ Ⓑ Ⓒ Ⓓ Ⓔ	9 Ⓐ Ⓑ Ⓒ Ⓓ Ⓔ	14 Ⓐ Ⓑ Ⓒ Ⓓ Ⓔ	19 Ⓐ Ⓑ Ⓒ Ⓓ Ⓔ	24 Ⓐ Ⓑ Ⓒ Ⓓ Ⓔ
5 Ⓐ Ⓑ Ⓒ Ⓓ Ⓔ	10 Ⓐ Ⓑ Ⓒ Ⓓ Ⓔ	15 Ⓐ Ⓑ Ⓒ Ⓓ Ⓔ	20 Ⓐ Ⓑ Ⓒ Ⓓ Ⓔ	25 Ⓐ Ⓑ Ⓒ Ⓓ Ⓔ

Section 5

1 Ⓐ Ⓑ Ⓒ Ⓓ Ⓔ	5 Ⓐ Ⓑ Ⓒ Ⓓ Ⓔ	9 Ⓐ Ⓑ Ⓒ Ⓓ Ⓔ	13 Ⓐ Ⓑ Ⓒ Ⓓ Ⓔ
2 Ⓐ Ⓑ Ⓒ Ⓓ Ⓔ	6 Ⓐ Ⓑ Ⓒ Ⓓ Ⓔ	10 Ⓐ Ⓑ Ⓒ Ⓓ Ⓔ	14 Ⓐ Ⓑ Ⓒ Ⓓ Ⓔ
3 Ⓐ Ⓑ Ⓒ Ⓓ Ⓔ	7 Ⓐ Ⓑ Ⓒ Ⓓ Ⓔ	11 Ⓐ Ⓑ Ⓒ Ⓓ Ⓔ	15 Ⓐ Ⓑ Ⓒ Ⓓ Ⓔ
4 Ⓐ Ⓑ Ⓒ Ⓓ Ⓔ	8 Ⓐ Ⓑ Ⓒ Ⓓ Ⓔ	12 Ⓐ Ⓑ Ⓒ Ⓓ Ⓔ	16 Ⓐ Ⓑ Ⓒ Ⓓ Ⓔ

Experimental Section – See page 11 for details.

Writing Sample

Schools would like to get to know you better through a story you tell using one of the ideas below. Please choose the idea you find most interesting and write a story using the idea as your first sentence. Please fill in the circle next to the one you choose.

Ⓐ I didn't expect to learn anything new, but . . .

Ⓑ I had fifteen minutes to solve the puzzle.

Use this page and the next page to complete your writing sample.

Continue on next page

SECTION 1
25 Questions

Following each problem in this section, there are five suggested answers. Work each problem in your head or in the blank space provided at the right of the page. Then look at the five suggested answers and decide which one is best.

<u>Note:</u> Figures that accompany problems in this section are drawn as accurately as possible EXCEPT when it is stated in a specific problem that its figure is not drawn to scale.

Sample Problem:

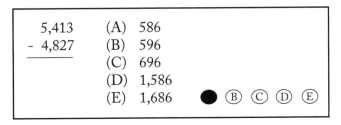

5,413	(A)	586
- 4,827	(B)	596
	(C)	696
	(D)	1,586
	(E)	1,686

USE THIS SPACE FOR FIGURING.

1. If $N + 5 = 5$, then $N =$

   (A) 0
   (B) $\frac{1}{5}$
   (C) 1
   (D) 5
   (E) 10

   $0 + 5 = 5$

---

2. If two dozen balloons are <u>divided equally among</u> <u>eight children</u>, how many balloons does each child get?

   (A) 2
   (B) 3
   (C) 4
   (D) 5
   (E) 6

   $8\overline{)24}$ → 3 $2 \times 12 = 24$

GO ON TO THE NEXT PAGE.

USE THIS SPACE FOR FIGURING.

<u>Questions 3-4</u> are based on the graph that shows the progress of a nonstop hike on a trail up to the top of a mountain that is 500 meters above sea level.

3. How many hours did the hikers take to reach the top of the mountain?

    (A) 4
    (B) 3
    (C) 2
    (D) 1
    (E) $\frac{1}{2}$

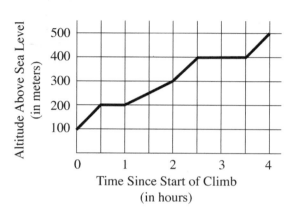

4. The hikers' altitude at the end of the hike up the mountain was how many meters greater than it was at the start of the hike?

    (A) 100
    (B) 200
    (C) 300
    (D) 400
    (E) 500

5. There are 1-cent, 5-cent, 10-cent, and 25-cent coins on a table. If Edith needs exactly 36 cents, what is the least number of coins she must take?

    (A) 2
    (B) 3
    (C) 5
    (D) 6
    (E) 9

    $10 + 25 + 1 = 36$

6. Which of the following numbers is divisible by 7?

    (A) 742
    (B) 734
    (C) 730
    (D) 726
    (E) 722

GO ON TO THE NEXT PAGE.

USE THIS SPACE FOR FIGURING.

7. The circle graph indicates how the average seventh grade student spends his or her 24-hour day. Approximately how many hours does the average seventh grade student spend on family time?

   (A) 1.3 hours
   (B) 1.9 hours
   (C) 2.4 hours
   (D) 2.9 hours
   (E) 3.1 hours

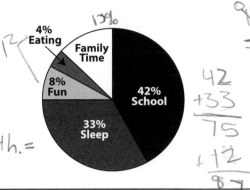

8. Jules paid for a book with a $20 bill and received x dollars in change. Which tells how many dollars he paid for the book?

   (A) $20x$
   (B) $\frac{x}{20}$
   (C) $\frac{20}{x}$
   (D) $20 + x$
   (E) $20 - x$

$$\begin{array}{r} {}^{1}6\,{}^{1}2\,8 \\ +\ 4\ \blacksquare\ 7 \\ \hline 1,\,1\,\triangle\,5 \end{array}$$

9. In the addition problem above, ■ can be which of the following digits?

   (A) 7
   (B) 5
   (C) 3
   (D) 1
   (E) 0

GO ON TO THE NEXT PAGE.

USE THIS SPACE FOR FIGURING.

10. Rose took a 3-mile walk and walked the first mile in 10 minutes. If she continued to walk at the same rate, what part of an hour did her walk take?

(A) $\frac{1}{6}$

(B) $\frac{1}{4}$

(C) $\frac{1}{3}$

(D) $\frac{1}{2}$

(E) $\frac{3}{4}$

11. A triangle has a perimeter of 57 inches. Side a is 3 inches shorter than twice side b, and side c is 4 inches longer than side b. How many inches long is side a?

(A) 10

(B) 14

(C) 18

(D) 24

(E) 25

12. Joe has 80 quarters. His sister has 25 quarters, 10 nickels, and 40 dimes. How much more money does Joe have than his sister?

(A) $4.25

(B) $8.75

(C) $9.25

(D) $10.25

(E) $13.75

13. If $\frac{x}{y}$ = 1 and neither x nor y equals zero, which of the following must be true?

(A) x is greater than y

(B) y is greater than x

(C) $x = y + 1$

(D) $x = 1$

(E) $x = y$

GO ON TO THE NEXT PAGE.

USE THIS SPACE FOR FIGURING.

14. At Banham School, five classes, each with 20 students, wish to form three clubs. If every student must belong to exactly one club and the membership of no club may outnumber the membership of another by more than one, what is the least possible number of students in one club?

   (A) 15
   (B) 20
   (C) 21
   (D) 33
   (E) 34

15. The cost of a long-distance telephone call is P cents for the first three minutes and Q cents for each additional minute. What is the cost, in cents, of a nine-minute call?

   (A) $P + (3 \times Q)$
   (B) $P + (6 \times Q)$
   (C) $(3 \times P) + (6 \times Q)$
   (D) $(3 \times P) + (9 \times Q)$
   (E) $9 \times (P + Q)$

16. Which fraction is closest to 37%?

   (A) $\frac{1}{4}$
   (B) $\frac{1}{3}$
   (C) $\frac{3}{8}$
   (D) $\frac{2}{5}$
   (E) $\frac{3}{7}$

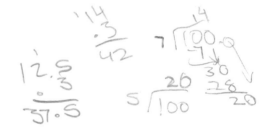

17. The perimeter of a rectangle measuring 3×8 units is equal to the

   (A) area of the same rectangle in square units
   (B) perimeter of a regular pentagon with side lengths of 3 units
   (C) area of a triangle with the base length of 3 units and height of 8 units
   (D) area in square units of a rectangle measuring 2 units by 11 units
   (E) area in square units of a square measuring 22 units on a side

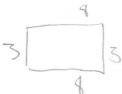

GO ON TO THE NEXT PAGE.

USE THIS SPACE FOR FIGURING.

18. Sophie is making bows for packages and uses 1.25m of ribbon per bow. If she has 12m of ribbon and makes as many bows as possible, how much ribbon will she have left?

(A) 0.6m

(B) 2.4m

(C) 0.72m

(D) 0.7m

(E) 0.75m

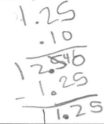

19. What is the average of 30, –30, 50, –20, –30, and 60?

(A) 10

(B) 60

(C) 44

(D) 12

(E) 15

20. In the figure shown, if *ABCD* is a square, the length of *CE* is 3, and the length of *EF* is 5, what is the area of rectangular region *ABEF*?

(A) 15

(B) 16

(C) 24

(D) 34

(E) 40

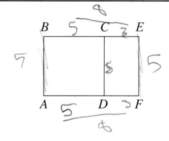

$$\frac{1}{2} \bigcirc \frac{1}{4} = N$$

21. The value of *N* will be greatest when which of the following symbols is put in the circle above?

(A) +

(B) –

(C) ×

(D) ÷

(E) The value of *N* will be the same for each of the symbols.

GO ON TO THE NEXT PAGE.

USE THIS SPACE FOR FIGURING.

22. To win the battle, Leigh Anne must give the number in at most two tries. Which two numbers should she give to be sure she will win?

    (A) 20 and 23
    (B) 33 and 48
    (C) 60 and 70
    (D) 64 and 66
    (E) 2,046 and 2,048

    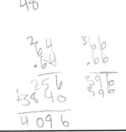

BATTLE OF THE MATH MINDS
When a number is multiplied by itself, the product is 4,096. What is the number?

23. The figure shows the dimensions of a rectangular block of wood. If the block were cut into two identical rectangular blocks, which of the following could be the dimensions, in centimeters, of each of the smaller blocks?

    (A) 8 × 6 × 2
    (B) 8 × 12 × 2
    (C) 4 × 6 × 2
    (D) 4 × 6 × 4
    (E) 4 × 12 × 2

    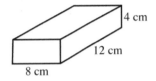

24. At the end of a race, Justin finished 2 meters ahead of Alex. Bob finished ahead of Justin but behind Josh. Tom finished 5 meters ahead of Alex and 2 meters behind Bob. If they were the first five to finish the race, who finished THIRD?

    (A) Justin
    (B) Alex
    (C) Bob
    (D) Josh
    (E) Tom

    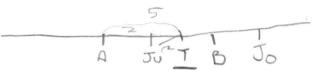

25. Which of the following pairs of numbers does NOT have an average equal to half the average of 8 and 16?

    (A) 2 and 4
    (B) 4 and 8
    (C) 5 and 7
    (D) 6 and 6
    (E) 12 and 0

STOP
**IF YOU FINISH BEFORE TIME IS CALLED,
YOU MAY CHECK YOUR WORK ON THIS SECTION ONLY.
DO NOT TURN TO ANY OTHER SECTION IN THE TEST.**

SECTION 2
40 Questions

Read each passage carefully and then answer the questions about it. For each question, decide on the basis of the passage which one of the choices best answers the question.

Piranha fish are widely known around the world. These fish have a reputation as being killers, but humans do not have much to fear from them. A lot of these stories come from the fact that the piranha feed in packs, so it seems as though they hunt in groups. It is true that their teeth are razor sharp and they can inflict a nasty bite on humans. They do
Line 5   not, however, hunt humans swimming in the water.

Sometimes known as the "vampire fish," the piranha is found in rivers and lakes around the Amazon River in South America. They are attracted by traces of blood in the water. Scout piranha in the pack will signal to the rest when there is food available, which starts a feeding frenzy. Because groups of fish can contain hundreds of members, they can
10   devour a meal very quickly.

In many areas, these fish are used as a food source by the locals, and they will even use the teeth to make tools and weapons. The locals have a respect for these fish and will be wary when around known piranha fish waters.

1. Piranha have a reputation for being killers because

    (A) their teeth are razor sharp
    (B) they can devour a meal very quickly
    (C) the local natives tell stories of attacks
    (D) they hunt humans swimming in water
    (E) they feed in large groups, so it looks like they hunt for food together

2. Piranha are sometimes known as "vampire fish" (line 6) because they

    (A) feed only at night
    (B) are related to rodents
    (C) suck blood out of their prey
    (D) are found in the Amazon River
    (E) are drawn to blood in the water

3. In line 13, the term "wary" most nearly means

    (A) cautious
    (B) afraid
    (C) quiet
    (D) nervous
    (E) upset

4. Which of the following is true of piranha?

    (A) They are inedible.
    (B) They hunt in packs.
    (C) They feed on blood.
    (D) They travel in packs.
    (E) They feed on humans.

5. According to the passage, all of the following about piranha are true EXCEPT

    (A) locals hunt them for food
    (B) they feed on humans
    (C) they live in rivers and lakes in South America
    (D) groups of fish can contain hundreds of members
    (E) scout piranha signal the pack when they find food

GO ON TO THE NEXT PAGE.

The myths of the ancient Greeks described the world as managed by a multitude of beings who were like men but who had different powers. They loved and hated and quarreled with each other, like men. They were gods, though, and could not kill each other because they were immortal. They were, however, subject to a higher power which they called Necessity.

Line 5

Many of the myths are beautiful, but some are not. They seem to say that the gods rose from savagery, just as men did, and were not always sure what was good and noble. The Greeks thought of the gods as friendly people, rather like themselves. They also feared them as terrible and strong and ready to punish those who angered them.

6. The author is primarily concerned with

   (A) discussing life in ancient Greece
   (B) telling a story involving the Greek gods
   (C) explaining the role of Necessity in Greek myths
   (D) describing the Greeks' belief about their gods
   (E) explaining why the Greeks believed in many gods

7. When the author mentions "beings" in the second sentence, he is referring to

   (A) the gods
   (B) Necessity
   (C) the Greek people
   (D) men and animals
   (E) people from different countries

8. The author suggests that the Greeks thought of their gods as

   (A) friendly but possibly dangerous
   (B) domineering and easily angered
   (C) cheerful and uninterested in men
   (D) easily surprised by men's behavior
   (E) dishonest and generally irresponsible

9. According to the passage, the Greek gods were subject to

   (A) the will of men
   (B) the will of other gods
   (C) good and noble judges
   (D) a power called Necessity
   (E) laws made by the gods themselves

10. The author concludes from the Greek myths that the gods were

   (A) evil
   (B) unkind
   (C) imperfect
   (D) unnecessary
   (E) unconcerned

GO ON TO THE NEXT PAGE.

Tenderly Kala nursed her little waif, wondering silently why it did not gain strength and agility as did the little apes of other mothers. It was nearly a year from the time the little fellow came into her possession before he would walk alone, and as for climbing—my, but how stupid he was!

Line 5 Kala sometimes talked with the older females about her young hopeful, but none of them could understand how a child could be so slow and backward in learning to care for itself. Why, it could not even find food alone, and more than twelve moons had passed since Kala had come upon it.

Had they known that the child had seen thirteen moons before it had come into

10 Kala's possession they would have considered its case as absolutely hopeless, for the little apes of their own tribe were as far advanced in two or three moons as was this little stranger after twenty-five. Tublat, Kala's husband, was sorely vexed, and but for the female's careful watching would have put the child out of the way.

"He will never be a great ape," he argued. "Always will you have to carry him and

15 protect him. What good will he be to the tribe? None; only a burden."

"Let us leave him quietly sleeping among the tall grasses, that you may bear other and stronger apes to guard us in our old age."

"Never, Broken Nose," replied Kala. "If I must carry him forever, so be it."

11. According to the passage, Kala has had the child for how many moons?

(A) two
(B) twelve
(C) three
(D) thirteen
(E) twenty-five

12. The author uses moons to emphasize all of the following EXCEPT the child's

(A) age
(B) shortcomings
(C) time with Kala
(D) physical growth
(E) dependence on Kala

13. Which word can be substituted for "vexed" (line 12) without changing the meaning of the statement?

(A) irate
(B) hesitant
(C) frustrated
(D) jealous
(E) contemplative

14. Which adjective best describes Kala's attitude toward the child?

(A) hopeless
(B) resigned
(C) diffident
(D) confused
(E) resolute

15. According to the passage, Tublat suggests abandoning the child for all of the following reasons EXCEPT that he

(A) is weak
(B) looks different
(C) requires extra care
(D) contributes nothing to the tribe
(E) will never distinguish himself

GO ON TO THE NEXT PAGE.

As in all phases of mountaineering, on snow and ice the judgment of the probable safety of the climb rests with the leader. He must be able to estimate the length of the climb, allowing for an early enough start to permit finishing. He must know at a glance if there is avalanche danger. He must instantly recognize those situations in which
Line 5 speed is essential. He must know whether the capabilities of his party will meet the test of a traverse across an ice slope. He must be alert to fatigue in others and adjust the pace accordingly, even calling retreat if the physical condition of a member of his group has deteriorated to the point wherein safety of the party may be jeopardized.

16. According to the author, the leader of a mountain climb may direct his party to retreat if a member of the party

   (A) wishes to stop
   (B) becomes extremely tired
   (C) travels at a very erratic pace
   (D) refuses to comply with group decisions
   (E) does not recognize a dangerous situation

17. It can be inferred that the most important characteristic of the leader of a mountain-climbing party is

   (A) great strength
   (B) good judgment
   (C) acrobatic agility
   (D) reckless courage
   (E) unusual endurance

18. Knowledge of which of the following is NOT mentioned by the author as being required of a leader of a mountain-climbing expedition?

   (A) the indications of a sudden snow slide
   (B) the approximate length of time the climb will require
   (C) the difficulties encountered by previous climbers of the mountain
   (D) the factors which make it necessary for the party to move more slowly
   (E) the factors which make it necessary for the party to move more quickly

19. As used in the passage, "deteriorated" (line 8) most likely means

   (A) crumbled
   (B) rusted
   (C) worsened
   (D) corrupted
   (E) consumed

20. Which of the following titles best summarizes the content of the passage?

   (A) Ideal Weather Conditions for a Mountain Climb
   (B) Cooperation and Coordination: Essentials for Climbing
   (C) Dangers on a Mountain Climb and How to Prevent Them
   (D) The Abilities Required of the Leader of a Mountain Climb
   (E) The Hazards of Mountaineering: Man's Greatest Challenge

GO ON TO THE NEXT PAGE.

Some "scientists" peering through microscopes thought they saw strange things which escaped their colleagues' notice. In 1836, Andrew Crosse actually believed he saw microscopic insects appearing as a by-product of his research. He had wanted to create minerals artificially by sending an electrical current through certain chemicals. Crosse
Line 5 recorded what he observed through his microscope—small, white projections growing from an electrified stone. He observed that, after he had electrified the stone, each projection became "a perfect insect, standing erect on a few bristles which formed its tail." Crosse reported that the smaller insects had six legs and the larger ones, eight. He guessed them to be a previously unobserved specimen genus *Arcurus*, and said they flew
10 about the laboratory, hiding in dark spots as though avoiding light.

In 1872, Bastian, a noted English biologist, also claimed to have witnessed spontaneous development of life in his microscope. But when colleagues repeated his experiments, taking precautions against bacteria in the air, the results were disappointing. In 1906, Burke, using radium, thought he had developed half-living,
15 half-crystalline forms which he called "radiobes." Other scientists, however, failed to confirm Burke's findings.

21. When Andrew Crosse began his experiments, he was trying to

(A) test the reactions of the genus *Arcurus* to light

(B) determine the number of legs characteristic of the genus *Arcurus*

(C) prove that microscopic insects grow from electrified minerals

(D) study certain minerals to determine their ability to conduct electrical current

(E) produce artificial minerals through the application of electrical current to chemicals

22. According to the passage, Burke classified a "radiobe" (line 15) as which of the following?

(A) a vegetable

(B) an animal

(C) a mineral

(D) part living and part non-living

(E) part vegetable and part animal

23. It can be inferred that the living forms that Bastian observed with his microscope were actually

(A) radiobe specimens

(B) members of the genus *Arcurus*

(C) multiplying bacteria in the air

(D) insects capable of standing on their tails

(E) projections from the electrified stone

24. Which of the following would the author probably believe best establishes the truth or falsehood of a scientist's claims?

(A) reading the scientist's notes

(B) repeating the scientist's original experiment

(C) checking the scientist's background and qualifications

(D) examining the scientist's equipment for defects

(E) studying the previous scientific investigation in the field

25. The passage is primarily concerned with

(A) proving that life cannot develop out of mineral matter

(B) describing how experiments can be carefully controlled

(C) showing how some scientists misunderstand what they see

(D) demonstrating that amateur scientists often are more successful than professionals

(E) criticizing scientists for failure to confirm the findings of Crosse, Bastian, and Burke

GO ON TO THE NEXT PAGE.

Women play an important part in the Hopi society. Although Hopi political leaders and warriors are traditionally men, both genders take part in storytelling, music and artwork, and traditional medicine. The fields, the crops, the pueblos, belong to women. Descent is traced through the women; a child belongs to its mother's clan.

Line 5 If a marriage is broken, women typically retain property rights.

Each clan is divided into "lineages" whose members are all descended from a common ancestor. The clan organizations extend across all the villages. Children are named by the women of the father's clan. On the twentieth day of a baby's life, the women of the paternal clan gather, and each woman brings a name and a gift for the

10 child. The parents select the name that will be used.

Hopi children learn all domestic skills from their mother. Boys learn to weave, while girls care for the infants, learn to grind corn, weave baskets, and make pottery. Each clan is in charge of certain religious ceremonies throughout the year. The spirits of natural elements, animals, or deceased ancestors, known as kachinas, are welcomed to

15 the village each spring to dance and sing, bring rain for the harvest, and give gifts to the children.

Prior to each kachina ceremony, the men spend days carefully carving masked dolls in the likeness of the kachina represented in that particular ceremony. Following the ceremony, the dolls are hung on the walls of the pueblo and are studied in order to

20 learn the characteristics of that certain kachina. The revered dolls are then passed on to the daughters of the village to give visual understanding to the spirits.

26. According to the passage, a woman is usually
    (A) the main storyteller
    (B) subjected to rule by men
    (C) the model for the kachina dolls
    (D) responsible for political leadership
    (E) considered the main property owner

27. If a Hopi marriage fails, the couple's fields are probably
    (A) confiscated by the clan
    (B) held in trust for the children
    (C) turned over to the entire tribe
    (D) kept in the wife's possession
    (E) reverted to the husband's family

28. A carved kachina doll is most like
    (A) a spiritual aide
    (B) a casual toy
    (C) a wall hanging
    (D) a member of the clan
    (E) the head of a ceremony

29. We can infer from the passage that kachinas are
    (A) feared by the children
    (B) deceased clan members
    (C) valued for their ability to dance
    (D) sacred spirits treasured by the tribe
    (E) chosen for their influence on the hunt

30. Which of the following best expresses the main idea of the passage?
    (A) The Hopis are governed by men.
    (B) Hopi men bring about the kachina ceremony.
    (C) Among the Hopi, women are of great importance.
    (D) Hopi children learn weaving from their mothers.
    (E) Hopi women are responsible for naming children.

GO ON TO THE NEXT PAGE.

In the dark the old man could feel the morning coming and as he rowed he heard the trembling sound as flying fish left the water and the hissing that their stiff set wings made as they soared away in the darkness. He was very fond of flying fish as they were his principal friends on the ocean. He was sorry for the birds, especially the small delicate dark

Line 5 terns that were always flying and looking and almost never finding, and he thought, the birds have a harder life than we do except for the robber birds and the heavy strong ones. Why did they make birds so delicate and fine as those sea swallows when the ocean can be so cruel? She is kind and very beautiful. But she can be so cruel and it comes so suddenly and such birds that fly, dipping and hunting, with their small sad voices are made too

10 delicately for the sea.

He always thought of the sea as *la mar* which is what people call her in Spanish when they love her. Sometimes those who love her say bad things of her but they are always said as though she were a woman. Some of the younger fishermen, those who used buoys as floats for their lines and had motorboats, bought when the shark livers had

15 brought much money, spoke of her as *el mar* which is masculine. They spoke of her as a contestant or a place or even an enemy. But the old man always thought of her as feminine and as something that gave or withheld great favours, and if she did wild or wicked things it was because she could not help them.

31. The old man believes most birds have a harder life than people because they

(A) are so delicate and fine
(B) live far from the smell of land
(C) fly, dipping and hunting, with sad voices
(D) have difficulty finding food on the open sea
(E) have stiff set wings that make a hissing sound as they soar away

32. According to the passage, when the shark livers brought much money, some fishermen spoke of the sea as

(A) an enemy
(B) an equal
(C) a female
(D) *la mar*
(E) a friend

33. It can be inferred that the old man

(A) is much too tired to row
(B) is ready to give up being a fisherman
(C) shares much in common with the younger fishermen
(D) is eager to have a younger fisherman join him in his boat
(E) sees the sea differently from some of the younger fishermen

34. The tone of the passage is one of

(A) remembrance
(B) worry
(C) anticipation
(D) frustration
(E) information

35. What is the main idea of the passage?

(A) people think differently about the sea
(B) the man respects and is one with the sea
(C) you are never alone when you are on the sea
(D) fishing in the early morning yields more fish
(E) the sea is complex with all of its animal life

GO ON TO THE NEXT PAGE.

Melanie's purse was pink suede, and the purple patches on it were beautiful, but Alex was very tired of it. A colorful, braided yarn bracelet finished off the handle and marked it as special; the bracelet greeted Alex whenever Melanie hung her bag on the back of her chair. It was there now. Thoughtfully, he took the bracelet's strand between *Line 5* his fingers, and, without disturbing Melanie, uncapped his black marker and doodled on it. He marked it with black lines and laid it out on his desk; though, a moment later when Melanie leaned forward, the bracelet moved off Alex's desk and its still-wet markings were able to add some picturesque touches to Melanie's suede purse.

36. According to the passage, which of the following statements is true?

(A) Alex's markings were on nothing but Melanie's bracelet.

(B) Alex drew on Melanie's bracelet just as she told him not to.

(C) Alex drew on Melanie's bracelet with marker and ripped her purse.

(D) Alex did not mean to draw on Melanie's bracelet with marker.

(E) Alex did not tell Melanie that he was drawing on her bracelet.

37. Melanie sits

(A) next to Alex

(B) behind Alex

(C) in front of Alex

(D) two seats away from Alex

(E) across the room from Alex

38. Alex found the sight of Melanie's purse

(A) tiresome

(B) beautiful

(C) terrifying

(D) refreshing

(E) ridiculous

39. At the time Alex doodled on her bracelet, Melanie was

(A) facing Alex

(B) standing up

(C) leaning back in her seat

(D) leaning forward over a book

(E) leaning over to pick up a pencil

40. Alex is best described as

(A) worried

(B) studious

(C) confused

(D) considerate

(E) mischievous

STOP

**IF YOU FINISH BEFORE TIME IS CALLED,
YOU MAY CHECK YOUR WORK ON THIS SECTION ONLY.
DO NOT TURN TO ANY OTHER SECTION IN THE TEST.**

SECTION 3
60 Questions

This section consists of two different types of questions: synonyms and analogies. There are directions and a sample question for each type.

Synonyms

Each of the following questions consists of one word followed by five words or phrases. You are to select the one word or phrase whose meaning is closest to the word in capital letters.

Sample Question:

CHILLY:
(A) lazy
(B) nice
(C) dry
(D) cold
(E) sunny   Ⓐ Ⓑ Ⓒ ● Ⓔ

---

1. TRADE:
   (A) tax
   (B) rush
   (C) advise
   (D) flatten
   (E) exchange

2. CALM:
   (A) hide
   (B) soothe
   (C) drain
   (D) thicken
   (E) borrow

3. DONATE:
   (A) give
   (B) divide
   (C) confine
   (D) govern
   (E) copy

4. PRICELESS:
   (A) accurate
   (B) reckless
   (C) doubtful
   (D) valuable
   (E) legal

5. SCARCE:
   (A) rare
   (B) evil
   (C) sudden
   (D) decayed
   (E) abandoned

6. THOROUGH:
   (A) actual
   (B) useful
   (C) complete
   (D) possible
   (E) new

7. SYMPATHIZE:
   (A) agree
   (B) befriend
   (C) ignore
   (D) observe
   (E) contaminate

8. AMBIANCE:
   (A) roundabout
   (B) atmosphere
   (C) temperament
   (D) precaution
   (E) doubt

GO ON TO THE NEXT PAGE.

9. MEMENTO:
   (A) script
   (B) badge
   (C) engraving
   (D) directory
   (E) souvenir

10. HOAX:
    (A) maze
    (B) dream
    (C) riddle
    (D) prank
    (E) puzzle

11. COLOSSAL:
    (A) sweet
    (B) smooth
    (C) huge
    (D) close
    (E) limp

12. AUTHENTIC:
    (A) written
    (B) ordinary
    (C) decided
    (D) real
    (E) ancient

13. CALAMITY:
    (A) rejection
    (B) detraction
    (C) disaster
    (D) restriction
    (E) penalty

14. EXHILARATE:
    (A) excite
    (B) display
    (C) expel
    (D) discuss
    (E) repeat

15. CONTRADICT:
    (A) destroy
    (B) release
    (C) reveal
    (D) damage
    (E) oppose

16. ENCUMBER:
    (A) repel
    (B) burden
    (C) agitate
    (D) disprove
    (E) disappoint

17. ADHERE:
    (A) leave
    (B) climb
    (C) detach
    (D) follow
    (E) remember

18. GLITCH:
    (A) error
    (B) denial
    (C) ejection
    (D) weakness
    (E) falsehood

19. MEDLEY:
    (A) mood
    (B) mastery
    (C) measure
    (D) mixture
    (E) motive

20. SUBTLE:
    (A) faint
    (B) harsh
    (C) known
    (D) blatant
    (E) insensitive

GO ON TO THE NEXT PAGE.

21. PROBABLE:

   (A) visible
   (B) classical
   (C) accidental
   (D) anticipated
   (E) combustible

22. INSTIGATE:

   (A) stir up
   (B) cry out
   (C) go along
   (D) try again
   (E) do without

23. ANTISOCIAL:

   (A) unbelievable
   (B) withdrawn
   (C) unremarkable
   (D) wicked
   (E) unlucky

24. IDIOSYNCRASY:

   (A) inquiring attitude
   (B) instinctive reaction
   (C) illogical conclusion
   (D) impressive cunning
   (E) individual peculiarity

25. ABSTAIN:

   (A) taunt
   (B) bother
   (C) tarnish
   (D) decline
   (E) wonder

26. FISSURE:

   (A) disorder
   (B) eruption
   (C) entrance
   (D) branch
   (E) crack

27. RETORT:

   (A) sharp answer
   (B) naive question
   (C) deafening shout
   (D) arrogant demand
   (E) convincing argument

28. ELATION:

   (A) convenience
   (B) appearance
   (C) exclusion
   (D) accuracy
   (E) delight

29. CANDID:

   (A) frank
   (B) literate
   (C) shallow
   (D) preserved
   (E) manageable

30. ANIMOSITY:

   (A) hostility
   (B) resistance
   (C) discomfort
   (D) exaggeration
   (E) embarrassment

GO ON TO THE NEXT PAGE.

Analogies

The following questions ask you to find relationships between words. For each question, select the answer choice that best completes the meaning of the sentence.

Sample Question:

> Kitten is to cat as
> (A) fawn is to colt
> (B) puppy is to dog
> (C) cow is to bull
> (D) wolf is to bear
> (E) hen is to rooster   (A)   (C) (D) (E)

Choice (B) is the best answer because a kitten is a young cat just as a puppy is a young dog. Of all the answer choices, (B) states a relationship that is most like the relationship between <u>kitten</u> and <u>cat</u>.

---

31. Polish is to shiny as wash is to

    (A) soft
    (B) clean
    (C) ready
    (D) dry
    (E) ironed

32. Battery is to flashlight as

    (A) juice is to orange
    (B) bolt is to wrench
    (C) gasoline is to car
    (D) hinge is to door
    (E) oven is to stove

33. Composer is to symphony as

    (A) architect is to building
    (B) magnate is to money
    (C) chef is to knife
    (D) conductor is to train
    (E) thief is to money

34. Seed is to sprout as

    (A) plant is to grow
    (B) garden is to weed
    (C) dawn is to morning
    (D) teenager is to infant
    (E) downpour is to trickle

35. Colony is to ants as

    (A) herd is to buffalo
    (B) stadium is to fans
    (C) zoo is to monkeys
    (D) town is to populace
    (E) shepherd is to flock

36. Shell is to egg as

    (A) seed is to peach
    (B) glove is to mitten
    (C) arm is to leg
    (D) planet is to sun
    (E) skull is to brain

37. Logo is to product as

    (A) phrase is to syntax
    (B) style is to fashion
    (C) tongue is to speech
    (D) label is to merchandise
    (E) correspondence is to manuscript

38. Hurl is to catch as

    (A) toss is to snag
    (B) throw is to aim
    (C) pass is to target
    (D) lob is to fumble
    (E) fling is to heave

GO ON TO THE NEXT PAGE.

39. Glare is to light as

    (A) stare is to vision
    (B) blare is to sound
    (C) blaze is to smoke
    (D) power is to steam
    (E) motion is to speed

40. Duck is to bird as

    (A) trout is to fish
    (B) stallion is to horse
    (C) pullet is to chicken
    (D) keyboard is to piano
    (E) shark is to hammerhead

41. Trivial is to useful as

    (A) pursuit is to track
    (B) compose is to write
    (C) convert is to helpful
    (D) bland is to distinctive
    (E) decline is to downfall

42. Jumbled is to objects as

    (A) nervous is to people
    (B) deranged is to places
    (C) marred is to contents
    (D) displeasing is to choices
    (E) bewildered is to thoughts

43. Photography is to images as

    (A) painting is to talent
    (B) sculpture is to forms
    (C) knitting is to dexterity
    (D) caricature is to etchings
    (E) statistics is to mathematics

44. Shelter is to protection as

    (A) pane is to window
    (B) bed is to blanket
    (C) picture is to wall
    (D) curtain is to privacy
    (E) lampshade is to brightness

45. Eternity is to time as

    (A) credulity is to love
    (B) deity is to religion
    (C) infinity is to number
    (D) community is to size
    (E) maternity is to motherhood

46. Concrete is to foundation as

    (A) wood is to beam
    (B) copper is to gold
    (C) walnut is to maple
    (D) steel is to hardness
    (E) stone is to solidness

47. Cabinet is to drawer as

    (A) house is to door
    (B) blanket is to bed
    (C) button is to jacket
    (D) wood is to splinter
    (E) mailbox is to letter

48. Hangar is to airplane as

    (A) signal is to train
    (B) runway is to landing
    (C) ocean is to steamship
    (D) turnpike is to hitchhiker
    (E) garage is to automobile

49. Kind is to indulgent as tolerant is to

    (A) jolly
    (B) lovable
    (C) graceful
    (D) enviable
    (E) permissive

50. Nervous is to jumpy as

    (A) remote is to zealous
    (B) excitable is to jittery
    (C) passionate is to aloof
    (D) ardent is to ambitious
    (E) outspoken is to reserved

GO ON TO THE NEXT PAGE.

51. Nonfiction is to biography as fiction is to
    (A) essay
    (B) history
    (C) novel
    (D) editorial
    (E) autobiography

52. Cockpit is to pilot as
    (A) cab is to trucker
    (B) forest is to ranger
    (C) mast is to mariner
    (D) bridge is to engineer
    (E) radio is to broadcaster

53. Contract is to individuals as
    (A) treaty is to nations
    (B) license is to permits
    (C) cohesion is to unions
    (D) marriage is to proposal
    (E) alliance is to permanence

54. Drowsy is to comatose as untidy is to
    (A) stern
    (B) slovenly
    (C) saturated
    (D) doubtful
    (E) dejected

55. Teacher is to assignment as doctor is to
    (A) disease
    (B) hospital
    (C) operation
    (D) stethoscope
    (E) prescription

56. Broker is to stocks as
    (A) monitor is to classes
    (B) realtor is to properties
    (C) astronaut is to spaceships
    (D) philosopher is to theories
    (E) physicist is to experiments

57. Kennel is to dog as
    (A) lair is to cat
    (B) zoo is to pig
    (C) school is to fish
    (D) hutch is to rabbit
    (E) cave is to vegetation

58. Blood is to artery as
    (A) horn is to bull
    (B) wine is to grape
    (C) chord is to piano
    (D) muscle is to bone
    (E) traffic is to tunnel

59. Humanitarian is to aid as
    (A) advisor is to counsel
    (B) debater is to business
    (C) entertainer is to circus
    (D) organizer is to society
    (E) evaluator is to computer

60. Soldier is to battalion as
    (A) leaf is to rake
    (B) wing is to bird
    (C) lake is to water
    (D) captain is to ship
    (E) planet is to galaxy

STOP
**IF YOU FINISH BEFORE TIME IS CALLED,
YOU MAY CHECK YOUR WORK ON THIS SECTION ONLY.
DO NOT TURN TO ANY OTHER SECTION IN THE TEST.**

SECTION 4
25 Questions

Following each problem in this section, there are five suggested answers. Work each problem in your head or in the blank space provided at the right of the page. Then look at the five suggested answers and decide which one is best.

<u>Note:</u> Figures that accompany problems in this section are drawn as accurately as possible EXCEPT when it is stated in a specific problem that its figure is not drawn to scale.

Sample Problem:

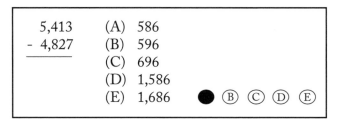

5,413	(A) 586
- 4,827	(B) 596
	(C) 696
	(D) 1,586
	(E) 1,686

● Ⓑ Ⓒ Ⓓ Ⓔ

USE THIS SPACE FOR FIGURING.

1. If all 25 students in a class went on a class trip, what percent of the students went on the trip?
   - (A) $\frac{1}{4}$%
   - (B) 1%
   - (C) 25%
   - (D) 50%
   - (E) 100%

---

2. 4,■86

   In the number above, the hundreds digit is covered by a box. If this number is less than 4,486, what is the largest digit that can be under the box?
   - (A) 0
   - (B) 3
   - (C) 4
   - (D) 7
   - (E) 9

---

3. If Joseph earned $232.00 for 32 hours of work, how much will he earn for 40 hours of work?
   - (A) $240.00
   - (B) $288.00
   - (C) $290.00
   - (D) $320.00
   - (E) $332.00

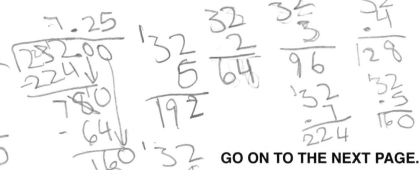

GO ON TO THE NEXT PAGE.

USE THIS SPACE FOR FIGURING.

4. Estimate: $\dfrac{998 \times 1{,}004}{48 \times 52}$

   (A) 40
   (B) 200
   (C) 400
   (D) 2,000
   (E) 4,000

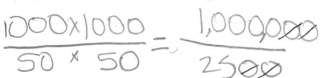

5. Ann swims six laps every five minutes. At that rate, how many laps does she swim in one hour?

   (A) 30
   (B) 36
   (C) 50
   (D) 60
   (E) 72

6. $\dfrac{1}{3}, \dfrac{2}{4}, \dfrac{3}{5}, \dfrac{4}{6}, \dfrac{5}{7}, \ldots \dfrac{10}{\square}$

   If the pattern above is continued as shown, $\square$ =

   (A) 12
   (B) 13
   (C) 14
   (D) 18
   (E) 30

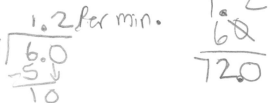

GO ON TO THE NEXT PAGE.

USE THIS SPACE FOR FIGURING.

<u>Questions 7-9</u> are based on the graph.

7. The original price of <u>model *P*</u> was <u>how much more than</u> the original price of model *S*?

   (A) $170
   (B) $300
   (C) $310
   (D) $320
   (E) $520

8. The original price of which model was reduced by about 50 percent?

   (A) *P*
   (B) *Q*
   (C) *R*
   (D) *S*
   (E) *T*

9. The tablet model that has the <u>highest</u> current price was <u>originally</u> introduced at a price of

   (A) $620
   (B) $520
   (C) $450
   (D) $300
   (E) $140

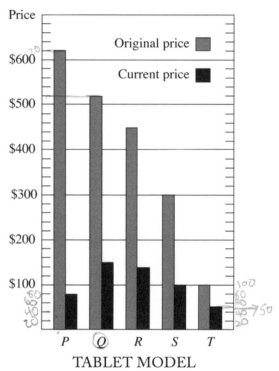

ORIGINAL PRICES AND CURRENT PRICES OF FIVE TABLETS

TABLET MODEL

10. What is the circumference of the largest circle that can be cut from a piece of paper with an area of 144 square inches?

    (A) 144π in.
    (B) 14π in.
    (C) 12π in.
    (D) 72π in.
    (E) 100π in.

11. $5 \times (\frac{1}{2} + \frac{1}{2}) =$

    (A) $\frac{5}{4}$
    (B) $\frac{7}{4}$
    (C) $\frac{5}{2}$
    (D) 5
    (E) 6

GO ON TO THE NEXT PAGE.

USE THIS SPACE FOR FIGURING.

12. Students at Celestial Middle School must wear uniforms. They may choose between a white, yellow, blue, or red shirt and navy, black, or khaki pants. Choosing randomly, what is the probability that a student will choose a red shirt AND navy pants?

    (A) $\frac{1}{3}$

    (B) $\frac{1}{4}$

    (C) $\frac{2}{7}$

    (D) $\frac{1}{12}$

    (E) $\frac{7}{12}$

13. If m is 4 more than k, then k must be

    (A) 4
    (B) $\frac{1}{4}$ of m
    (C) 4 less than m
    (D) 4 times m
    (E) 4 more than m

$$
\begin{array}{r}
482 \\
\times 23 \\
\hline
1446 \\
\longrightarrow 964 \\
\end{array}
$$

14. In the partly completed multiplication problem above, what is the value of the digit 9 on the line with the arrow?

    (A) 9
    (B) 90
    (C) 900
    (D) 9,000
    (E) 90,000

15. $\frac{1}{2}$ of which expression is greatest?

    (A) $N - 2$
    (B) $N - 1$
    (C) N
    (D) $N + 1$
    (E) $N + 2$

GO ON TO THE NEXT PAGE.

USE THIS SPACE FOR FIGURING.

16. The figure shown shows the face of a square card that has two small holes punched in it. If the card is turned face down, it CANNOT look like which of the following?

(A)

(B)

(C)

(D)

(E)

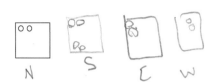

17. If $(7 \times N) + 3 = 6$, then $N =$

(A) $\frac{3}{7}$

(B) $\frac{9}{7}$

(C) 3

(D) 7

(E) 14

18. In the figure, rods of lengths 6 centimeters, 8 centimeters, and 10 centimeters overlap by 2 centimeters where they are connected. If the overall length is N centimeters, then $N =$

(A) 18

(B) 20

(C) 22

(D) 24

(E) 26

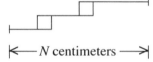

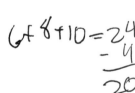

19. If $N + 5$ is greater than 7, then $2 \times N$ MUST be greater than

(A) 4

(B) 6

(C) 8

(D) 10

(E) 12

GO ON TO THE NEXT PAGE.

USE THIS SPACE FOR FIGURING.

20. A rectangular package of baseballs is packed tightly in rows with 2 baseballs in each row. If the radius of each baseball is 3 cm, what are the dimensions of the rectangular package?

(A) 12 cm × 18 cm

(B) 2 cm × 3 cm

(C) 6 cm × 9 cm

(D) 18 cm × 18 cm

(E) 12 cm × 9 cm

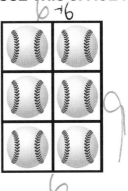

21. If $\textcircled{x} = x^2 + 1$, then $\textcircled{3} =$

(A) 4

(B) 6

(C) 7

(D) 10

(E) 16

22. If the length of a rectangle is 3 times the width, w, what is the perimeter in terms of w?

(A) $2(3 + w)$

(B) $4(3 + w)$

(C) $3w$

(D) $4w$

(E) $8w$

23. The decimal numeral $\square.3$ is equal to which fraction?

(A) $\dfrac{(10 \times \square) + 3}{10}$

(B) $\dfrac{10 \times (\square + 3)}{10}$

(C) $\dfrac{\square + 3}{10}$

(D) $\dfrac{(100 \times \square) + 3}{100}$

(E) $\dfrac{\square + 3}{100}$

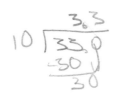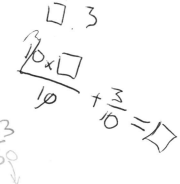

GO ON TO THE NEXT PAGE.

USE THIS SPACE FOR FIGURING.

24. A triangle has vertices located at the points $(3, 2)$, $(3, 9)$, and $(7, 2)$ on the coordinate plane. Find its area.

    (A) 10.5 square units
    (B) 14.0 square units
    (C) 18.0 square units
    (D) 28.0 square units
    (E) 31.5 square units

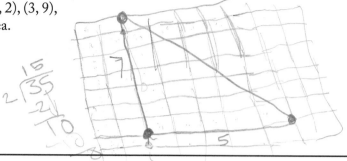

25. Calculate: $3 + 6 * 2^3 \div 3 + 3^2$

    (A) 6
    (B) 8
    (C) 28
    (D) 30
    (E) 33

STOP
**IF YOU FINISH BEFORE TIME IS CALLED,
YOU MAY CHECK YOUR WORK ON THIS SECTION ONLY.
DO NOT TURN TO ANY OTHER SECTION IN THE TEST.**

Be sure each mark completely fills the answer space.
Start with number 1 for each new section of the test. You may find more answer spaces than you need.
If so, please leave them blank.

Section 1

1 Ⓐ Ⓑ Ⓒ Ⓓ Ⓔ	6 Ⓐ Ⓑ Ⓒ Ⓓ Ⓔ	11 Ⓐ Ⓑ Ⓒ Ⓓ Ⓔ	16 Ⓐ Ⓑ Ⓒ Ⓓ Ⓔ	21 Ⓐ Ⓑ Ⓒ Ⓓ Ⓔ
2 Ⓐ Ⓑ Ⓒ Ⓓ Ⓔ	7 Ⓐ Ⓑ Ⓒ Ⓓ Ⓔ	12 Ⓐ Ⓑ Ⓒ Ⓓ Ⓔ	17 Ⓐ Ⓑ Ⓒ Ⓓ Ⓔ	22 Ⓐ Ⓑ Ⓒ Ⓓ Ⓔ
3 Ⓐ Ⓑ Ⓒ Ⓓ Ⓔ	8 Ⓐ Ⓑ Ⓒ Ⓓ Ⓔ	13 Ⓐ Ⓑ Ⓒ Ⓓ Ⓔ	18 Ⓐ Ⓑ Ⓒ Ⓓ Ⓔ	23 Ⓐ Ⓑ Ⓒ Ⓓ Ⓔ
4 Ⓐ Ⓑ Ⓒ Ⓓ Ⓔ	9 Ⓐ Ⓑ Ⓒ Ⓓ Ⓔ	14 Ⓐ Ⓑ Ⓒ Ⓓ Ⓔ	19 Ⓐ Ⓑ Ⓒ Ⓓ Ⓔ	24 Ⓐ Ⓑ Ⓒ Ⓓ Ⓔ
5 Ⓐ Ⓑ Ⓒ Ⓓ Ⓔ	10 Ⓐ Ⓑ Ⓒ Ⓓ Ⓔ	15 Ⓐ Ⓑ Ⓒ Ⓓ Ⓔ	20 Ⓐ Ⓑ Ⓒ Ⓓ Ⓔ	25 Ⓐ Ⓑ Ⓒ Ⓓ Ⓔ

Section 2

1 Ⓐ Ⓑ Ⓒ Ⓓ Ⓔ	9 Ⓐ Ⓑ Ⓒ Ⓓ Ⓔ	17 Ⓐ Ⓑ Ⓒ Ⓓ Ⓔ	25 Ⓐ Ⓑ Ⓒ Ⓓ Ⓔ	33 Ⓐ Ⓑ Ⓒ Ⓓ Ⓔ
2 Ⓐ Ⓑ Ⓒ Ⓓ Ⓔ	10 Ⓐ Ⓑ Ⓒ Ⓓ Ⓔ	18 Ⓐ Ⓑ Ⓒ Ⓓ Ⓔ	26 Ⓐ Ⓑ Ⓒ Ⓓ Ⓔ	34 Ⓐ Ⓑ Ⓒ Ⓓ Ⓔ
3 Ⓐ Ⓑ Ⓒ Ⓓ Ⓔ	11 Ⓐ Ⓑ Ⓒ Ⓓ Ⓔ	19 Ⓐ Ⓑ Ⓒ Ⓓ Ⓔ	27 Ⓐ Ⓑ Ⓒ Ⓓ Ⓔ	35 Ⓐ Ⓑ Ⓒ Ⓓ Ⓔ
4 Ⓐ Ⓑ Ⓒ Ⓓ Ⓔ	12 Ⓐ Ⓑ Ⓒ Ⓓ Ⓔ	20 Ⓐ Ⓑ Ⓒ Ⓓ Ⓔ	28 Ⓐ Ⓑ Ⓒ Ⓓ Ⓔ	36 Ⓐ Ⓑ Ⓒ Ⓓ Ⓔ
5 Ⓐ Ⓑ Ⓒ Ⓓ Ⓔ	13 Ⓐ Ⓑ Ⓒ Ⓓ Ⓔ	21 Ⓐ Ⓑ Ⓒ Ⓓ Ⓔ	29 Ⓐ Ⓑ Ⓒ Ⓓ Ⓔ	37 Ⓐ Ⓑ Ⓒ Ⓓ Ⓔ
6 Ⓐ Ⓑ Ⓒ Ⓓ Ⓔ	14 Ⓐ Ⓑ Ⓒ Ⓓ Ⓔ	22 Ⓐ Ⓑ Ⓒ Ⓓ Ⓔ	30 Ⓐ Ⓑ Ⓒ Ⓓ Ⓔ	38 Ⓐ Ⓑ Ⓒ Ⓓ Ⓔ
7 Ⓐ Ⓑ Ⓒ Ⓓ Ⓔ	15 Ⓐ Ⓑ Ⓒ Ⓓ Ⓔ	23 Ⓐ Ⓑ Ⓒ Ⓓ Ⓔ	31 Ⓐ Ⓑ Ⓒ Ⓓ Ⓔ	39 Ⓐ Ⓑ Ⓒ Ⓓ Ⓔ
8 Ⓐ Ⓑ Ⓒ Ⓓ Ⓔ	16 Ⓐ Ⓑ Ⓒ Ⓓ Ⓔ	24 Ⓐ Ⓑ Ⓒ Ⓓ Ⓔ	32 Ⓐ Ⓑ Ⓒ Ⓓ Ⓔ	40 Ⓐ Ⓑ Ⓒ Ⓓ Ⓔ

Section 3

1 Ⓐ Ⓑ Ⓒ Ⓓ Ⓔ	13 Ⓐ Ⓑ Ⓒ Ⓓ Ⓔ	25 Ⓐ Ⓑ Ⓒ Ⓓ Ⓔ	37 Ⓐ Ⓑ Ⓒ Ⓓ Ⓔ	49 Ⓐ Ⓑ Ⓒ Ⓓ Ⓔ
2 Ⓐ Ⓑ Ⓒ Ⓓ Ⓔ	14 Ⓐ Ⓑ Ⓒ Ⓓ Ⓔ	26 Ⓐ Ⓑ Ⓒ Ⓓ Ⓔ	38 Ⓐ Ⓑ Ⓒ Ⓓ Ⓔ	50 Ⓐ Ⓑ Ⓒ Ⓓ Ⓔ
3 Ⓐ Ⓑ Ⓒ Ⓓ Ⓔ	15 Ⓐ Ⓑ Ⓒ Ⓓ Ⓔ	27 Ⓐ Ⓑ Ⓒ Ⓓ Ⓔ	39 Ⓐ Ⓑ Ⓒ Ⓓ Ⓔ	51 Ⓐ Ⓑ Ⓒ Ⓓ Ⓔ
4 Ⓐ Ⓑ Ⓒ Ⓓ Ⓔ	16 Ⓐ Ⓑ Ⓒ Ⓓ Ⓔ	28 Ⓐ Ⓑ Ⓒ Ⓓ Ⓔ	40 Ⓐ Ⓑ Ⓒ Ⓓ Ⓔ	52 Ⓐ Ⓑ Ⓒ Ⓓ Ⓔ
5 Ⓐ Ⓑ Ⓒ Ⓓ Ⓔ	17 Ⓐ Ⓑ Ⓒ Ⓓ Ⓔ	29 Ⓐ Ⓑ Ⓒ Ⓓ Ⓔ	41 Ⓐ Ⓑ Ⓒ Ⓓ Ⓔ	53 Ⓐ Ⓑ Ⓒ Ⓓ Ⓔ
6 Ⓐ Ⓑ Ⓒ Ⓓ Ⓔ	18 Ⓐ Ⓑ Ⓒ Ⓓ Ⓔ	30 Ⓐ Ⓑ Ⓒ Ⓓ Ⓔ	42 Ⓐ Ⓑ Ⓒ Ⓓ Ⓔ	54 Ⓐ Ⓑ Ⓒ Ⓓ Ⓔ
7 Ⓐ Ⓑ Ⓒ Ⓓ Ⓔ	19 Ⓐ Ⓑ Ⓒ Ⓓ Ⓔ	31 Ⓐ Ⓑ Ⓒ Ⓓ Ⓔ	43 Ⓐ Ⓑ Ⓒ Ⓓ Ⓔ	55 Ⓐ Ⓑ Ⓒ Ⓓ Ⓔ
8 Ⓐ Ⓑ Ⓒ Ⓓ Ⓔ	20 Ⓐ Ⓑ Ⓒ Ⓓ Ⓔ	32 Ⓐ Ⓑ Ⓒ Ⓓ Ⓔ	44 Ⓐ Ⓑ Ⓒ Ⓓ Ⓔ	56 Ⓐ Ⓑ Ⓒ Ⓓ Ⓔ
9 Ⓐ Ⓑ Ⓒ Ⓓ Ⓔ	21 Ⓐ Ⓑ Ⓒ Ⓓ Ⓔ	33 Ⓐ Ⓑ Ⓒ Ⓓ Ⓔ	45 Ⓐ Ⓑ Ⓒ Ⓓ Ⓔ	57 Ⓐ Ⓑ Ⓒ Ⓓ Ⓔ
10 Ⓐ Ⓑ Ⓒ Ⓓ Ⓔ	22 Ⓐ Ⓑ Ⓒ Ⓓ Ⓔ	34 Ⓐ Ⓑ Ⓒ Ⓓ Ⓔ	46 Ⓐ Ⓑ Ⓒ Ⓓ Ⓔ	58 Ⓐ Ⓑ Ⓒ Ⓓ Ⓔ
11 Ⓐ Ⓑ Ⓒ Ⓓ Ⓔ	23 Ⓐ Ⓑ Ⓒ Ⓓ Ⓔ	35 Ⓐ Ⓑ Ⓒ Ⓓ Ⓔ	47 Ⓐ Ⓑ Ⓒ Ⓓ Ⓔ	59 Ⓐ Ⓑ Ⓒ Ⓓ Ⓔ
12 Ⓐ Ⓑ Ⓒ Ⓓ Ⓔ	24 Ⓐ Ⓑ Ⓒ Ⓓ Ⓔ	36 Ⓐ Ⓑ Ⓒ Ⓓ Ⓔ	48 Ⓐ Ⓑ Ⓒ Ⓓ Ⓔ	60 Ⓐ Ⓑ Ⓒ Ⓓ Ⓔ

Section 4

1 Ⓐ Ⓑ Ⓒ Ⓓ Ⓔ	6 Ⓐ Ⓑ Ⓒ Ⓓ Ⓔ	11 Ⓐ Ⓑ Ⓒ Ⓓ Ⓔ	16 Ⓐ Ⓑ Ⓒ Ⓓ Ⓔ	21 Ⓐ Ⓑ Ⓒ Ⓓ Ⓔ
2 Ⓐ Ⓑ Ⓒ Ⓓ Ⓔ	7 Ⓐ Ⓑ Ⓒ Ⓓ Ⓔ	12 Ⓐ Ⓑ Ⓒ Ⓓ Ⓔ	17 Ⓐ Ⓑ Ⓒ Ⓓ Ⓔ	22 Ⓐ Ⓑ Ⓒ Ⓓ Ⓔ
3 Ⓐ Ⓑ Ⓒ Ⓓ Ⓔ	8 Ⓐ Ⓑ Ⓒ Ⓓ Ⓔ	13 Ⓐ Ⓑ Ⓒ Ⓓ Ⓔ	18 Ⓐ Ⓑ Ⓒ Ⓓ Ⓔ	23 Ⓐ Ⓑ Ⓒ Ⓓ Ⓔ
4 Ⓐ Ⓑ Ⓒ Ⓓ Ⓔ	9 Ⓐ Ⓑ Ⓒ Ⓓ Ⓔ	14 Ⓐ Ⓑ Ⓒ Ⓓ Ⓔ	19 Ⓐ Ⓑ Ⓒ Ⓓ Ⓔ	24 Ⓐ Ⓑ Ⓒ Ⓓ Ⓔ
5 Ⓐ Ⓑ Ⓒ Ⓓ Ⓔ	10 Ⓐ Ⓑ Ⓒ Ⓓ Ⓔ	15 Ⓐ Ⓑ Ⓒ Ⓓ Ⓔ	20 Ⓐ Ⓑ Ⓒ Ⓓ Ⓔ	25 Ⓐ Ⓑ Ⓒ Ⓓ Ⓔ

Section 5

Experimental Section – See page 11 for details.

Writing Sample

Schools would like to get to know you better through a story you tell using one of the ideas below. Please choose the idea you find most interesting and write a story using the idea as your first sentence. Please fill in the circle next to the one you choose.

Ⓐ I thought it was going to be another normal day, until…

Ⓑ All I wanted was a glass of water.

Use this page and the next page to complete your writing sample.

Continue on next page

SECTION 1
25 Questions

Following each problem in this section, there are five suggested answers. Work each problem in your head or in the blank space provided at the right of the page. Then look at the five suggested answers and decide which one is best.

Note: Figures that accompany problems in this section are drawn as accurately as possible EXCEPT when it is stated in a specific problem that its figure is not drawn to scale.

Sample Problem:

5,413	(A) 586
- 4,827	(B) 596
	(C) 696
	(D) 1,586
	(E) 1,686 ● Ⓑ Ⓒ Ⓓ Ⓔ

USE THIS SPACE FOR FIGURING.

1. What is the next number in the series 3, 6, 11, 18, __?

    (A) 24
    (B) 25
    (C) 26
    (D) 27
    (E) 28

2. If there are 150 calories in a $\frac{1}{2}$-cup serving, how many calories are there in a 1-cup serving?

    (A) 75
    (B) 225
    (C) 300
    (D) 450
    (E) 600

3. About how much will three note pads cost if the sale price is $0.79 each?

    (A) $2.70
    (B) $2.40
    (C) $2.10
    (D) $1.80
    (E) $1.60

GO ON TO THE NEXT PAGE.

USE THIS SPACE FOR FIGURING.

4. If $N + 7 = 7$, then $N + 12 =$

    (A) 12
    (B) 7
    (C) 5
    (D) 1
    (E) 0

5. Which sum is closest to $39 + 18 + 42$?

    (A) $40 + 20 + 50$
    (B) $40 + 20 + 40$
    (C) $40 + 10 + 40$
    (D) $30 + 20 + 40$
    (E) $30 + 10 + 40$

6. The temperature was x degrees in the morning.
    What was the temperature, in degrees, after it went up
    two degrees and down five degrees?

    (A) $x - 10$
    (B) $x - 7$
    (C) $x - 3$
    (D) $x + 3$
    (E) $x + 7$

7. Which set of numbers is in order from least to greatest?

    (A) $\frac{7}{9}, \frac{3}{4}, 0.7, 0.8$
    (B) $0.7, 0.8, \frac{3}{4}, \frac{7}{9}$
    (C) $0.7, \frac{3}{4}, \frac{7}{9}, 0.8$
    (D) $0.7, \frac{3}{4}, 0.8, \frac{7}{9}$
    (E) $0.8, \frac{7}{9}, \frac{3}{4}, 0.7$

GO ON TO THE NEXT PAGE.

USE THIS SPACE FOR FIGURING.

8. Paul is at the corner of Broad Street and Main Street as shown in the figure. If he walks two blocks east and three blocks north, he will be at point

   (A) *A*
   (C) *C*
   (D) *D*
   (E) *E*

STREET MAP OF MAPLE CITY

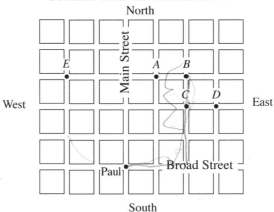

9. Which of the following sets of numbers contains only prime numbers?

   (A) 2, 3, 5, 7, 11
   (B) 3, 7, 11, 13, 15
   (C) 0, 1, 2, 3, 5
   (D) 5, 10, 15, 20, 25
   (E) 1, 2, 3, 4, 5

10. Ellen put 150 guppies in a tank that held 50 liters of water. She should only have two guppies for each liter of water. How many guppies should she remove from the tank?

    (A) 125
    (B) 100
    (C) 75
    (D) 50
    (E) 25

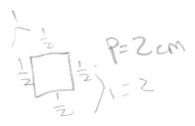

11. If the perimeter of a square is 2 centimeters, then the length of each side of the square is

    (A) 8 cm
    (B) 4 cm
    (C) 1 cm
    (D) $\frac{1}{2}$ cm
    (E) $\frac{1}{4}$ cm

GO ON TO THE NEXT PAGE.

USE THIS SPACE FOR FIGURING.

12. $40 \overline{)\blacksquare}$

The answer to the problem above will be between 4 and 5 if $\blacksquare$ is

(A) 360
(B) 181
(C) 150
(D) 9
(E) 4.5

13. A taxi ride from the airport costs $14 for one or two people and $3 more for each additional person. If four people share the cost of a taxi equally, how much does each pay?

(A) $4.25
(B) $5.00
(C) $5.75
(D) $6.00
(E) $8.50

14. If $\frac{n}{3}$ is a whole number, then n could be

(A) 343
(B) 353
(C) 403
(D) 473
(E) 483

15. Which figure can be drawn without lifting the pencil or retracing?

(A)

(B)

(C)

(D)

(E)

GO ON TO THE NEXT PAGE.

USE THIS SPACE FOR FIGURING.

16. Sylvia is taller than Georgio but shorter than David. Eric is taller than both Sylvia and Georgio. Who is tallest?

    (A) Georgio
    (B) Sylvia
    (C) Eric
    (D) David
    (E) It cannot be determined from the information given.

Questions 17-18 refer to the chart.

Students in a seventh-grade class were asked to identify their favorite recording artists.

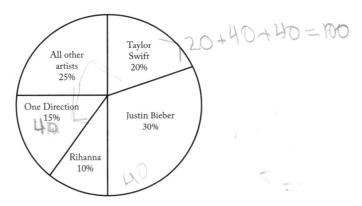

17. If there are 80 students in the class, how many of them prefer One Direction?

    (A) 10
    (B) 12
    (C) 15
    (D) 27
    (E) 65

18. How many more students preferred Justin Bieber to Rihanna?

    (A) 10
    (B) 16
    (C) 20
    (D) 30
    (E) 32

GO ON TO THE NEXT PAGE.

USE THIS SPACE FOR FIGURING.

19. In the problem $(3a + 5)a$, distributing a will result in
    (A) $4a + 5$
    (B) $4a + 5a$
    (C) $4a + 5 + a$
    (D) $3a^2 + 5$
    (E) $3a^2 + 5a$

20. A team that plays sixteen games in a season has won eight and lost three to date. What is the greatest number of games it can lose during the rest of the season and still win more than half of the games for the season?
    (A) 1
    (B) 2
    (C) 3
    (D) 4
    (E) 5

21. Solve the equation $-23 - (-2x) = -17$
    (A) $x = -20$
    (B) $x = -3$
    (C) $x = 3$
    (D) $x = 6$
    (E) $x = 15$

22. The square floor shown in the figure is to have tile on the shaded part and carpeting on the unshaded part. If the two parts are rectangular, what will be the ratio of the area of the tiled part to the area of the carpeted part?

    (A) $\frac{1}{20}$

    (B) $\frac{1}{5}$

    (C) $\frac{1}{4}$

    (D) $\frac{4}{5}$

    (E) It cannot be determined from the information given.

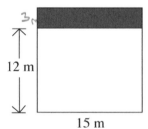

12 m

15 m

Figure not drawn to scale.

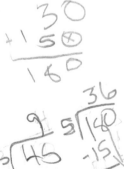

GO ON TO THE NEXT PAGE.

USE THIS SPACE FOR FIGURING.

23. If the positive whole number N is multiplied by a number less than 1, the answer MUST be

(A) less than N

(B) less than 1

(C) 0

(D) between 0 and 1

(E) greater than N

24. On the first day of Luke's fitness plan, he did 30 push-ups. On the second day, he did 45 push-ups. What was the percent increase in Luke's push-ups from the first to the second day?

(A) 15%

(B) $33\frac{1}{3}$%

(C) 45%

(D) 50%

(E) 75%

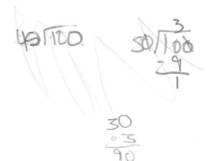

25. The average weight of three boys is 44 kilograms. If two of the boys gain 3 kilograms each and the other boy stays the same, what will their average weight be?

(A) 49 kg

(B) 48 kg

(C) 47 kg

(D) 46 kg

(E) 45 kg

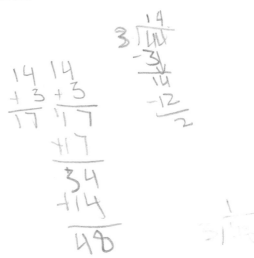

STOP
**IF YOU FINISH BEFORE TIME IS CALLED,
YOU MAY CHECK YOUR WORK ON THIS SECTION ONLY.
DO NOT TURN TO ANY OTHER SECTION IN THE TEST.**

SECTION 2
40 Questions

Read each passage carefully and then answer the questions about it. For each question, decide on the basis of the passage which one of the choices best answers the question.

> In the late 1970s, the Food and Drug Administration (FDA) approved the first vaccine that successfully prevented pneumococcal pneumonia. Researchers found that the rate that pneumonia occurs increases as we get older. In 2012, the FDA approved a new vaccine for adults 50 and older. This vaccine protects against thirteen strains
>
> *Line 5* of pneumococcal bacteria, which cause meningitis, pneumonia, and ear infections. The FDA said that 300,000 adults 50 years and older are hospitalized every year for pneumococcal pneumonia. Initial distribution was being aimed at persons over 65.
>
> "Despite the wide use of antibiotics, pneumonia today is the sixth leading cause of death in the United States," an FDA representative said. "The type of pneumonia
>
> *10* against which the vaccine protects accounts for a major portion of these deaths. The vaccine is effective in at least 80 percent of the people who receive it." Still, all these years later, the vaccine is a safe and effective way to prevent pneumonia.

1. This passage is primarily about
   (A) the first vaccine invented
   (B) leading causes of death
   (C) a vaccine for pneumonia
   (D) illness in the United States
   (E) the Food and Drug Administration

2. From the passage, it can be concluded that the vaccine approved in the late 1970s probably
   (A) increased the authority of the FDA
   (B) made the use of antibiotics obsolete
   (C) reduced the number of deaths from pneumonia
   (D) provided protection against illnesses other than pneumonia
   (E) raised health expenses for people in the United States

3. Which of the following could be substituted for "occurs" (line 3) without changing the meaning of the sentence?
   (A) falls out
   (B) breaks in
   (C) comes down
   (D) bursts forth
   (E) presents itself

4. According to the passage, pneumococcal bacteria cause all of the following EXCEPT
   (A) pneumonia
   (B) meningitis
   (C) infections
   (D) influenza
   (E) hospitalizations

5. The style of the passage is most like that found in
   (A) a textbook
   (B) an almanac
   (C) a news article
   (D) an encyclopedia
   (E) an advertisement

GO ON TO THE NEXT PAGE.

octopie

With the invention of new diving equipment, scientists have been able to study animals such as the octopus in their ocean habitats. Investigators have given tests to octopuses and found that their intelligence is high compared to that of other mollusks.

Line 5   In one interesting test, a live lobster was placed in a glass jar. In the mouth of the jar there was a cork stopper in which a small hole had been drilled. The jar was taken to sea and put in front of the entrance to the dwelling of an octopus. Octopuses like to eat lobsters, so in spite of the fact that it was surrounded by cameras, lights, and interested divers, the octopus came out and threw itself upon the lobster. When it discovered that it could not reach its prey, it turned red with anger and surprise, for the octopus shows

10   its emotions by changing color.

Normally, the octopus would have been able to paralyze its victim with the poison from its salivary glands. But it could see the lobster was still moving around inside the jar. It became very impatient and began to explore the jar. The octopus then found the hole in the cork stopper and squeezed its arm inside. When the tip of the arm touched

15   the lobster and the lobster moved, the octopus looked electrified. It seemed to realize that the stopper could be moved and in a few minutes it had pulled the stopper out of the jar with one arm and collected the lobster with two others.

6. The major purpose of the experiment described in the passage was to

(A) test how the octopus solves problems
(B) discover how the octopus poisons its victims
(C) study the emotions displayed by an octopus
(D) discover whether the octopus attacks lobsters
(E) observe how the octopus behaves when surrounded by divers

7. According to the passage, what was the octopus' first reaction to the lobster?

(A) exploring the jar
(B) pulling out the cork
(C) eating it immediately
(D) throwing itself on the jar
(E) pushing its arm through the hole

8. The octopus shows its emotions by

(A) changing color
(B) waving its arms
(C) hiding in caves
(D) secreting poison
(E) attacking its enemies

9. It is implied in the passage that the octopus came out of its home because it

(A) was attracted by the lights
(B) wanted to capture the lobster
(C) was frightened by the cameras
(D) was interested in the scientists
(E) wanted to play with the divers

10. It can be inferred from the passage that the octopus "looked electrified" (line 15) because it

(A) was caught by the divers
(B) was surprised and excited
(C) had become very frightened
(D) had been electrically shocked
(E) had been pinched by the lobster

GO ON TO THE NEXT PAGE.

In the whole world there can be no more dreary view than that from the northern slope of the Sierra Blanco. As far as the eye can reach stretches the great flat plain-land, all dusted over with patches of alkali, and intersected by clumps of the dwarfish chaparral bushes. On the extreme verge of the horizon lie a long chain of mountain peaks, with

Line 5 their rugged summits flecked with snow. In this great stretch of country there is no sign of life, nor of anything appertaining to life. There is no bird in the steel-blue heaven, no movement upon the dull, grey earth—above all, there is absolute silence. Listen as one may, there is no shadow of a sound in all that mighty wilderness; nothing but silence— complete and heart-subduing silence.

10 It has been said there is nothing appertaining to life upon the broad plain. That is hardly true. Looking down from the Sierra Blanco, one sees a pathway traced out across the desert, which winds away and is lost in the extreme distance. It is rutted with wheels and trodden down by the feet of many adventurers. Here and there are scattered white objects which glisten in the sun, and stand out against the dull deposit of alkali.

15 Approach, and examine them! They are bones: some large and coarse, others smaller and more delicate. The former have belonged to oxen, and the latter to men. For fifteen hundred miles one may trace this ghastly caravan route by these scattered remains of those who had fallen by the wayside.

11. The passage suggests that travelers died as the result of

(A) enemy attack
(B) violent storms
(C) wild animals
(D) disease or pestilence
(E) heat and lack of water

12. The word "rutted" (line 12) means

(A) ditched
(B) gated
(C) mated
(D) closed
(E) furrowed

13. In the second paragraph, the tone of the author is best described as

(A) angry
(B) ironic
(C) excited
(D) indifferent
(E) surprised

14. The most important function of the second paragraph is to emphasize that

(A) this is a desert wilderness
(B) life exists on the Sierra Blanco plain
(C) many lives were lost crossing this desert
(D) only the bravest explorers should traverse this area
(E) carving roads through desert is dangerous work

15. The author of this passage is primarily concerned with

(A) retracing the path of previous explorers
(B) telling the story of an ill-fated caravan journey
(C) emphasizing the bleakness of this desolate landscape
(D) proving life can be found on the Sierra Blanco plain
(E) describing the effects of alkali on bushes and bones

GO ON TO THE NEXT PAGE.

I wandered lonely as a cloud
That floats on high o'er vales and hills,
When all at once I saw a crowd,
A host, of golden daffodils, Beside the lake, beneath the trees,
Line 5   Fluttering and dancing in the breeze.

Continuous as the stars that shine
And twinkle on the Milky Way.
They stretched in never-ending line
Along the margin of a bay.
10   Ten thousand saw I at a glance,
Tossing their heads in sprightly dance.

The waves beside them danced, but they
Out-did the sparkling waves in glee.
A poet could not but be gay,
15   In such a jocund company.
I gazed—and gazed—but little thought
What wealth the show to me had brought.

For oft, when on my couch I lie
In vacant or in pensive mood,
20   They flash upon that inward eye
Which is the bliss of solitude,
And then my heart with pleasure fills,
And dances with the daffodils.

16. The poet uses which technique to describe the daffodils?

   (A) parable
   (B) irony
   (C) persuasion
   (D) alliteration
   (E) personification

17. Which of the following words could be substituted for "sprightly" (line 11) ?

   (A) weary
   (B) irksome –
   (C) energetic +
   (D) ambitious +
   (E) interesting +

18. "Jocund" (line 15) most nearly means

   (A) fancy
   (B) cheerful
   (C) touching
   (D) humorless
   (E) heartbroken

19. The tone of the last stanza can be described as both

   (A) wistful and happy
   (B) childish and candid
   (C) proud and indignant
   (D) confident and comical
   (E) sarcastic and despairing

20. Which of the following best describes the main idea of the poem?

   (A) You should always be envious of the beauty of nature.
   (B) Flowers can often remind you of unpleasant past events.
   (C) Ocean waves can remind you of flowers moving with a breeze.
   (D) Gazing at the Milky Way can never replace the joy that flowers can bring.
   (E) Nature provides so much peace and joy that even the memory of nature can make you happy.

GO ON TO THE NEXT PAGE.

Through the noonday heat they waited, their energy draining away bit by bit under the merciless sun. As the hours went by, Daniel's foreboding deepened. This waiting was not the same as the times he had crouched behind a rock eager for Raymond's signal. It was no flimsily-guarded caravan they awaited, but a group of real

Line 5   soldiers. And behind him was no tight-knit band that would move with precision and cunning, only a cluster of untried boys. Even now, as he glanced up, the flutter of a coat sleeve betrayed one of them. Still, he could count on them. He knew that every boy in the band was prepared to give his life. It was up to him, the one they had chosen leader, to see that none of them had to.

21. At the beginning of the passage, Daniel's attitude is one of deep

(A) pride
(B) sorrow
(C) disgust
(D) ignorance
(E) uneasiness

22. The effect of the sun on the waiting boys was to

(A) give them courage
(B) drain their energy
(C) make them optimistic
(D) make them livelier but more frightened of their task
(E) confuse them and make them believe that Raymond was signaling

23. The author mentions that "the flutter of a coat sleeve betrayed one of them" (lines 6-7) to show that Daniel's boys were

(A) inexperienced
(B) dishonest
(C) patriotic
(D) angry
(E) hurried

24. The fact that Daniel knew that every boy in the band was prepared to give his life made him realize that he

(A) was an unpopular leader
(B) lacked sympathy for the band
(C) was reluctant to give his own life
(D) felt that attacking the soldiers was cruel
(E) carried a great responsibility because he was their leader

25. Which of the following best describes the mood created by the author in the passage?

(A) anxious suspense
(B) intense activity
(C) boredom
(D) optimism
(E) grief

GO ON TO THE NEXT PAGE.

In China my grandmother loved the theater (which I, having been brought up in America, would not have been able to understand because of my limited vocabulary). When the actors came to the village and set up their scaffolding, my grandmother bought a large space up front. She would stay days and nights sleeping under the stars.

Line 5   Unfortunately, there was danger that bandits, who followed the actors, would make raids on households thinned out during performances.

"But, Grandmother," the family complained, "the bandits will steal the tables while we're gone." The family took the chairs to plays.

"I want every last one of you at that theater. I don't want to watch that play by
10   myself. How can I laugh all by myself? You want me to clap alone, is that it? I want everybody there."

"The robbers will ransack the food."

"So let them. Cook up the food and take it to the theater. If you're so worried about bandits, leave the doors open. Leave the windows open. Leave the house wide
15   open. We are going to the theater without worries."

So they left the doors open, and my whole family went to watch the actors. Sure enough, that night the bandits struck—not the house, but the theater. "Bandits!" the audience screamed. "Bandits!" the actors screamed. My family ran in all directions. When my grandmother and mother made their way home, the rest of the family was
20   home safe, proof to my grandmother that our family was immune to harm as long as they went to plays. They went to many plays after that.

26. According to the passage, the narrator does not
    (A) fear bandits
    (B) like school
    (C) like to cook
    (D) like to go to the theater
    (E) understand Chinese very well

27. It can be inferred from the passage that the plays were presented in
    (A) the home of one of the actors
    (B) a remote part of the village
    (C) the narrator's home
    (D) an outdoor area
    (E) the village school

28. The "scaffolding" mentioned in line 3 can best be interpreted to mean
    (A) a temporary stage
    (B) seats for the playgoers
    (C) dressing rooms for the actors
    (D) the framework of a building
    (E) partitions for the cast to wait behind

29. The family most likely took their chairs to the theater because
    (A) Grandmother wanted the chairs with her
    (B) the chairs were the family's most valuable possession
    (C) the theater had no seats
    (D) the bandits could not then steal them
    (E) the chairs were worth more than the tables

30. Grandmother's attitude toward the bandits can best be described as
    (A) nonchalant
    (B) indulgent
    (C) inquisitive
    (D) considerate
    (E) intolerant

GO ON TO THE NEXT PAGE.

Firewood can rarely be acquired at no cost, even if one considers only out-of-pocket costs. For those who cut and haul their own wood, there is at least the cost of gasoline and oil for the chain saw and truck. If the chain saw is used principally for cutting firewood for personal use, its cost is an indirect cost of the wood. Other

Line 5 hidden costs of heating with wood may include the need for a space to store the wood, protection of the wood from rain and snow, chimney cleaning, stovepipe replacement, and stove refinishing.

Many people heat with wood without being aware of or caring whether it is economical. Whether or not purely economic arguments favor wood heating, there

10 can be considerable enjoyment in heating with wood–from the physical exercise, from watching the fire, from the beauty of a wood stove, from the feeling of independence from the outside world for heating energy, and from the awareness that a renewable energy source is being used. In addition to these benefits, wood heating often does save money, especially if the wood is gathered rather than purchased, or if the wood heat replaces other sources of heat.

31. Which of the following would be the most appropriate title for the passage?

(A) Why Wood Fuel is a Better Bargain
(B) How to Achieve Energy Independence
(C) The Problems of Operating a Wood Stove
(D) Some Costs and Compensations of Heating with Wood
(E) Equipment Needed for Obtaining Firewood for Personal Use

32. The passage mentions all of the following items associated with firewood EXCEPT

(A) an ax
(B) a truck
(C) gasoline
(D) a chain saw
(E) storage space

33. By describing wood as a "renewable energy source" (lines 12-13), the author means that

(A) it is easy to cut and haul more wood whenever it is needed
(B) the physical exercise of getting firewood renews one's energy
(C) the fire in a wood stove can be renewed as desired
(D) new trees can be grown to replace those used for firewood
(E) energy independence is a renewing experience

34. With which of the following statements would the author be most likely to agree?

(A) Woodburning does not pollute the air as much as other means of heating.
(B) One should only heat with wood if it can be obtained at no cost.
(C) Electric heat is the most efficient kind of heat for most homes.
(D) Wood heating costs more than many people realize.
(E) The trouble and expense of getting wood make it an impractical fuel.

35. The passage lists all of the following reasons why many people use firewood EXCEPT the

(A) unavailability of other fuels
(B) pleasure of watching the fire
(C) attractiveness of wood stoves
(D) satisfaction of energy independence
(E) value of the exercise involved in getting wood

36. The author's tone in this passage can best be described as

(A) disillusioned
(B) explanatory
(C) nostalgic
(D) flippant
(E) cautious

GO ON TO THE NEXT PAGE.

> What really launched the nineteenth-century feminist crusade was the desire on the part of women to participate in the movement for the abolition of slavery. The refusal to admit women to the existing antislavery societies or even to permit them to speak in public for the cause led to defiance on the part of such women as Lucretia
>
> *Line 5* Mott. Barred from existing organizations, women abolitionists formed a national organization of their own in 1834. So great was the opposition that in 1838 a mob burned the hall in which the women were meeting. The next year the issue of admitting women to the national antislavery society of men broke up the organization into two movements, one composed of men alone, and one in which women cooperated with men on equal terms.

37. The main idea of the passage is that
    - (A) women formed some of the earliest antislavery societies
    - (B) the abolitionist movement broke up into two separate movements
    - (C) men were violently opposed to the nineteenth-century feminists
    - (D) the desire of women to fight slavery led to the nineteenth-century feminist movement
    - (E) the nineteenth-century feminists cooperated with men to oppose slavery

38. The style of the passage is most like that found in a
    - (A) novel
    - (B) diary
    - (C) biography
    - (D) history text
    - (E) short story

39. As used in the passage, the word "crusade" (line 1) most nearly means
    - (A) career
    - (B) caucus
    - (C) campaign
    - (D) ceremony
    - (E) convention

40. According to the passage, which of the following took place in 1839?
    - (A) Lucretia Mott was not allowed to speak in public.
    - (B) A mob burned the hall in which the women abolitionists were meeting.
    - (C) The men's antislavery society split into two groups.
    - (D) Women formed their own antislavery society.
    - (E) Women refused to participate in the men's antislavery society.

STOP
**IF YOU FINISH BEFORE TIME IS CALLED,
YOU MAY CHECK YOUR WORK ON THIS SECTION ONLY.
DO NOT TURN TO ANY OTHER SECTION IN THE TEST.**

SECTION 3
60 Questions

This section consists of two different types of questions: synonyms and analogies. There are directions and a sample question for each type.

Synonyms
Each of the following questions consists of one word followed by five words or phrases. You are to select the one word or phrase whose meaning is closest to the word in capital letters.

Sample Question:

> CHILLY:
>
> (A) lazy
> (B) nice
> (C) dry
> (D) cold
> (E) sunny   Ⓐ Ⓑ Ⓒ ● Ⓔ

---

1. BENEFICIAL:

   (A) amusing
   (B) pathetic
   (C) helpful
   (D) modern
   (E) festive

2. VISIBLE:

   (A) overhead
   (B) at home
   (C) in sight
   (D) very strong
   (E) understandable

3. SECURE:

   (A) crazy
   (B) kind
   (C) dusty
   (D) safe
   (E) ugly

4. ACCOMPANY:

   (A) sort out
   (B) give to
   (C) go with
   (D) copy from
   (E) provide for

5. AGGRAVATE:

   (A) steal
   (B) stop
   (C) catch
   (D) bother
   (E) reduce

6. MUTE:

   (A) harsh
   (B) silent
   (C) distant
   (D) gradual
   (E) orderly

7. PROPHESY:

   (A) reward
   (B) seminar
   (C) approval
   (D) prediction
   (E) contradiction

8. IMPOVERISH:

   (A) enrich
   (B) increase
   (C) bankrupt
   (D) improvise
   (E) incorporate

GO ON TO THE NEXT PAGE.

9. COARSE:
   (A) crude
   (B) stingy
   (C) musical
   (D) colorful
   (E) stretched

10. WARY:
   (A) tiring
   (B) hopeful
   (C) cautious
   (D) elegant
   (E) yielding

11. CLASH:
   (A) collision
   (B) formation
   (C) destination
   (D) progression
   (E) examination

12. ROBUST:
   (A) bionic
   (B) hardy
   (C) injured
   (D) defiant
   (E) bulbous

13. BLEND:
   (A) turn
   (B) spill
   (C) mash
   (D) mold
   (E) mingle

14. ERODE:
   (A) look in
   (B) snap off
   (C) clean up
   (D) fold over
   (E) wear away

15. LODGING:
   (A) dwelling
   (B) service
   (C) degree
   (D) range
   (E) roof

16. SUBDUE:
   (A) hoard
   (B) borrow
   (C) conquer
   (D) descend
   (E) underlie

17. TIMID:
   (A) small
   (B) frantic
   (C) dull
   (D) unknown
   (E) fainthearted

18. EQUITABLE:
   (A) fair
   (B) partial
   (C) wealthy
   (D) intelligent
   (E) unfinished

19. INCENTIVE:
   (A) decision
   (B) reputation
   (C) agreement
   (D) observance
   (E) motivation

20. PRECLUDE:
   (A) avoid
   (B) prevent
   (C) proceed
   (D) surrender
   (E) anticipate

GO ON TO THE NEXT PAGE.

21. EXONERATE:

   (A) incarcerate
   (B) accept
   (C) excuse
   (D) retire
   (E) return

22. PRECOCIOUS:

   (A) bad
   (B) erratic
   (C) valuable
   (D) advanced
   (E) dangerous

23. SPECTER:

   (A) ghost
   (B) beggar
   (C) volunteer
   (D) criminal
   (E) manager

24. STIFLE:

   (A) hit
   (B) push
   (C) corrupt
   (D) smother
   (E) frighten

25. LANGUID:

   (A) sly
   (B) listless
   (C) mellow
   (D) puzzled
   (E) effortless

26. PHILANTHROPY:

   (A) greed
   (B) cruelty
   (C) dwelling
   (D) generosity
   (E) diplomacy

27. MEDITATE:

   (A) injure
   (B) require
   (C) ponder
   (D) approve
   (E) contain

28. CONVERSATION:

   (A) chat
   (B) rain
   (C) group
   (D) poetry
   (E) refusal

29. EXTRACT:

   (A) let go
   (B) take out
   (C) breathe in
   (D) gulp down
   (E) change over

30. APPROPRIATE:

   (A) odd
   (B) suitable
   (C) faithful
   (D) unaware
   (E) noticeable

GO ON TO THE NEXT PAGE.

Analogies

The following questions ask you to find relationships between words. For each question, select the answer choice that best completes the meaning of the sentence.

Sample Question:

> Kitten is to cat as
> (A) fawn is to colt
> (B) puppy is to dog
> (C) cow is to bull
> (D) wolf is to bear
> (E) hen is to rooster   Ⓐ ● Ⓒ Ⓓ Ⓔ

Choice (B) is the best answer because a kitten is a young cat just as a puppy is a young dog. Of all the answer choices, (B) states a relationship that is most like the relationship between <u>kitten</u> and <u>cat</u>.

---

31. Ship is to life jacket as airplane is to
    (A) parachute
    (B) passenger
    (C) earphones
    (D) glider
    (E) wing

32. Clydesdale is to horse as Siamese is to
    (A) pig
    (B) cat
    (C) weasel
    (D) panther
    (E) pheasant

33. Worm is to tubular as
    (A) pie is to circular
    (B) tire is to conical
    (C) log is to squarish
    (D) egg is to rectangular
    (E) shoe is to cylindrical

34. Sheriff is to subpoena as orator is to
    (A) song
    (B) castigation
    (C) speech
    (D) orifice
    (E) medicine

35. Bouquet is to flowers as
    (A) fruit is to seeds
    (B) writing is to novels
    (C) sculpture is to artists
    (D) platoon is to soldiers
    (E) theater is to directors

36. Strengthened is to exercise as skilled is to
    (A) sport
    (B) speed
    (C) practice
    (D) accuracy
    (E) technique

37. Calendar is to day as
    (A) week is to year
    (B) clock is to hour
    (C) wrist is to watch
    (D) time is to motion
    (E) second is to minute

38. Deduct is to subtract as probable is to
    (A) often
    (B) usual
    (C) likely
    (D) reliable
    (E) definite

GO ON TO THE NEXT PAGE.

39. Computer is to mind as
    (A) key is to lock
    (B) collar is to neck
    (C) wheel is to spoke
    (D) telescope is to eye
    (E) architect is to building

40. Ring is to jewelry as
    (A) sock is to shoe
    (B) shirt is to cape
    (C) gem is to value
    (D) shirt is to clothing
    (E) rhinestone is to diamond

41. Knight is to armor as lobster is to
    (A) shell
    (B) sand
    (C) clam
    (D) pearl
    (E) ocean

42. Volcano is to lava as
    (A) spring is to well
    (B) geyser is to water
    (C) sprinkler is to hose
    (D) sprayer is to nozzle
    (E) fountain is to source

43. Toaster is to appliance as
    (A) bee is to insect
    (B) tree is to forest
    (C) plug is to socket
    (D) sentence is to report
    (E) refrigerator is to kitchen

44. Botanist is to plants as
    (A) bovine is to cows
    (B) equestrian is to horses
    (C) calligrapher is to books
    (D) anthropologist is to trees
    (E) ophthalmologist is to eyes

45. Shelf is to table as
    (A) desk is to chair
    (B) chart is to wall
    (C) crater is to bowl
    (D) desert is to oasis
    (E) mountain is to cabin

46. Cumulus is to cloud as
    (A) lake is to pond
    (B) bud is to flower
    (C) antenna is to insect
    (D) mountain is to valley
    (E) cottonmouth is to snake

47. Broadcasting is to speech as
    (A) edition is to corrections
    (B) publication is to writing
    (C) termination is to printing
    (D) authorship is to copyright
    (E) manuscript is to document

48. Blinded is to vision as abashed is to
    (A) attraction
    (B) stoutness
    (C) pessimism
    (D) awkwardness
    (E) self-confidence

49. Strive is to attain as
    (A) explain is to select
    (B) argue is to persuade
    (C) control is to execute
    (D) adapt is to emphasize
    (E) collaborate is to clarify

50. Wheel is to circle as
    (A) cog is to gear
    (B) lever is to lift
    (C) globe is to orb
    (D) switch is to current
    (E) pyramid is to antiquity

GO ON TO THE NEXT PAGE.

51. Doctor is to prescription as
    (A) car is to driver
    (B) author is to story
    (C) nurse is to surgery
    (D) plumber is to faucet
    (E) musician is to instrument

52. Apathy is to feeling as exhaustion is to
    (A) sleep
    (B) effort
    (C) warmth
    (D) solitude
    (E) comfort

53. Antiseptic is to infection as
    (A) admittance is to restraint
    (B) extraction is to destruction
    (C) suppression is to disturbance
    (D) distortion is to misinterpretation
    (E) admonishment is to appeasement

54. Marsupial is to kangaroo as herbivore is to
    (A) lion
    (B) tiger
    (C) bear
    (D) shark
    (E) elephant

55. Banish is to embrace as
    (A) expel is to invite
    (B) exile is to spurn
    (C) illness is to absence
    (D) remove is to eliminate
    (E) accept is to acknowledge

56. Reluctant is to eager as
    (A) ice is to fire
    (B) curious is to interested
    (C) calm is to foreboding
    (D) hesitant is to agreeable
    (E) plodding is to committed

57. Doll is to toy as
    (A) coffee is to tea
    (B) apple is to fruit
    (C) flower is to daisy
    (D) kite is to airplane
    (E) coloring books are to board games

58. Moat is to trench as
    (A) king is to crown
    (B) turret is to tower
    (C) horse is to saddle
    (D) sword is to shield
    (E) lance is to tournament

59. Fork is to pitchfork as spoon is to
    (A) combine
    (B) plow
    (C) shovel
    (D) scythe
    (E) mower

60. Banjo is to instrument as biography is to
    (A) story
    (B) article
    (C) fiction
    (D) editorial
    (E) autobiography

STOP
**IF YOU FINISH BEFORE TIME IS CALLED,
YOU MAY CHECK YOUR WORK ON THIS SECTION ONLY.
DO NOT TURN TO ANY OTHER SECTION IN THE TEST.**

SECTION 4
25 Questions

Following each problem in this section, there are five suggested answers. Work each problem in your head or in the blank space provided at the right of the page. Then look at the five suggested answers and decide which one is best.

<u>Note</u>: Figures that accompany problems in this section are drawn as accurately as possible EXCEPT when it is stated in a specific problem that its figure is not drawn to scale.

Sample Problem:

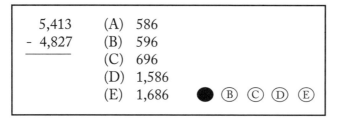

5,413	(A)	586
- 4,827	(B)	596
	(C)	696
	(D)	1,586
	(E)	1,686

● Ⓑ Ⓒ Ⓓ Ⓔ

USE THIS SPACE FOR FIGURING.

1. If $500 + 100 + \square + \blacktriangle = 668$, what does $\square + \blacktriangle$ equal?

(A) 8
(B) 60
(C) 68
(D) 600
(E) It cannot be determined from the information given.

2. Round 45.61849 to the nearest thousandth.

(A) 45.61
(B) 45.618
(C) 45.619
(D) 45.6184
(E) 45.6185

GO ON TO THE NEXT PAGE.

USE THIS SPACE FOR FIGURING.

3. In which of the following figures will a <u>triangle</u> be formed if *T* and *S* are joined by a straight line?

(A)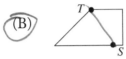

(B)

(C)

(D)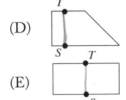

(E)

---

4. Which set of numbers will all be equal if rounded to the nearest tenth?

(A) 3.15, 3.23, 3.18, 3.209
(B) 4.36, 4.41, 4.45, 4.409
(C) 5.09, 5.14, 5.149, 5.15
(D) 6.17, 6.08, 6.05, 6.14
(E) 7.91, 7.95, 7.88, 7.85

---

5. If $200 + a = 800$, then $400 + a =$

(A) 1,600
(B) 1,400
(C) 1,200
(D) 1,000
(E) 600

---

6. If $17 + 17 + 17 + 17 + 17 + 17 = 6 \times \square$, what number goes in the $\square$?

(A) 6
(B) 17
(C) 62
(D) 87
(E) 102

GO ON TO THE NEXT PAGE.

USE THIS SPACE FOR FIGURING.

7. $\frac{1}{3} \div \frac{1}{3} =$

   (A) 0

   (B) $\frac{1}{9}$

   (C) $\frac{1}{3}$

   (D) 1

   (E) 9

$\frac{1}{3} \times \frac{3}{1} = \frac{3}{3} = 1$

8. If 10 percent of a number is 40, then 20 percent of the same number is

   (A) 8

   (B) 20

   (C) 25

   (D) 50

   (E) 80

$.1 \text{ of } x = 40$

$\frac{40}{1} \cdot \frac{10}{1} = 400$

400×2 ... 80.0

9. Pat is stringing beads in the pattern one yellow, one red, one blue, one green, and one white. The 64th bead will be what color?

   (A) yellow

   (B) red

   (C) blue

   (D) green

   (E) white

YRBGW ×13 −1

5 × 13 = 65

10. Josh is half as old as his sixteen year old sister, Lisa. How old will Josh be when Lisa is twenty years old?

   (A) 4

   (B) 6

   (C) 20

   (D) 12

   (E) 36

$20 - 16 = 4$

$+ 4$

12

$2\sqrt{16}$

GO ON TO THE NEXT PAGE.

USE THIS SPACE FOR FIGURING.

11.

Number Trick	
Step 1	Pick a number greater than 0. 3
Step 2	Multiply the number by 4. 12
Step 3	Add 8. 20
Step 4	Take 50%. 10
Step 5	Add 2. 12
Step 6	?
	The answer is 6.

Which of the following is Step 6 in the number trick above?

(A) Subtract 12.

(B) Multiply by 3.

(C) Add the number picked.

(D) Subtract the number picked.

(E) Subtract twice the number picked.

12. How many eighths are there in $2\frac{3}{8}$?

(A) 19

(B) 13

(C) 8

(D) 5

(E) 3

$\frac{19}{8}$

13. Order the following from least to greatest:

76%, 0.54, $\frac{1}{2}$, 35%, $\frac{3}{4}$, 0.92

(A) 35%, 76%, 0.54, $\frac{1}{2}$, $\frac{3}{4}$, 0.92

(B) $\frac{1}{2}$, $\frac{3}{4}$, 35%, 0.54, 76%, 0.92

(C) $\frac{1}{2}$, 35%, $\frac{3}{4}$, 0.54, 76%, 0.92

(D) 0.54, 0.92, $\frac{1}{2}$, $\frac{3}{4}$, 35%, 76%

(E) 35%, $\frac{1}{2}$, 0.54, $\frac{3}{4}$, 76%, 0.92

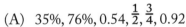

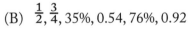

GO ON TO THE NEXT PAGE.

USE THIS SPACE FOR FIGURING.

14. What is the area of the figure?

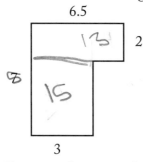

Figure not drawn to scale.

(A) 18.5 sq. units
(B) 27 sq. units
(C) 28 sq. units
(D) 34 sq. units
(E) 27.5 sq. units

15. On a certain test, 15 students answered more than 10 questions correctly and eight students answered at least 12 questions correctly. How many students answered exactly 11 questions correctly?

(A) 3
(B) 4
(C) 5
(D) 7
(E) 9

16. Reduce, or simplify, $\frac{15}{60}$ to lowest terms.

(A) $\frac{1}{4}$
(B) $\frac{3}{20}$
(C) $\frac{1}{3}$
(D) $\frac{3}{12}$
(E) 0.25

GO ON TO THE NEXT PAGE.

USE THIS SPACE FOR FIGURING.

17. The rectangle in the figure has six squares and the area of each square is 3. What is the area of the shaded region?

    (A) 6

    (B) $7\frac{1}{2}$

    (C) 9

    (D) $10\frac{1}{2}$

    (E) 12

18. The sum of three consecutive even numbers is 258. What is the smallest number?

    (A) 82

    (B) 84

    (C) 85

    (D) 86

    (E) 88

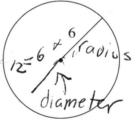

19. In the figure, the distance from the center of the circle to any point on the circle is 6. Which could NOT be the length of any line segment that lies inside the circle?

    (A) 13

    (B) 9

    (C) 8

    (D) 6

    (E) 4

GO ON TO THE NEXT PAGE.

USE THIS SPACE FOR FIGURING.

20. The fractional part of the number of biologists employed in education in year X was approximately

(A) $\frac{1}{4}$

(B) $\frac{7}{20}$

(C) $\frac{1}{2}$

(D) $\frac{3}{5}$

(E) $\frac{7}{10}$

$$\frac{35}{100} \div 5 = \frac{7}{20}$$

$$\frac{45}{100} = \frac{\square}{20}$$

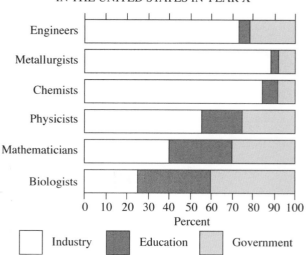

HOW SCIENTISTS AND ENGINEERS WERE EMPLOYED IN THE UNITED STATES IN YEAR X

Engineers
Metallurgists
Chemists
Physicists
Mathematicians
Biologists

Percent

☐ Industry   ■ Education   ▨ Government

21. The dimensions of a rectangular living room are 20 ft. by 18 ft. How many square yards of carpeting are needed to cover the floor?

(A) 40

(B) 45

(C) 90

(D) 240

(E) 360

22. The shaded region in the figure shown is divided by lines K, L, M, and S. The area between K and M is 45 square meters, between L and S is 40 square meters, and between M and S is 25 square meters. What is the area, in square meters, between K and L?

(A) 20

(B) 30

(C) 35

(D) 60

(E) 110

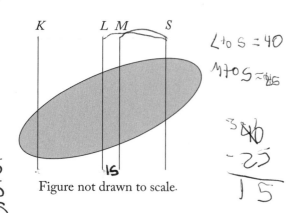

Figure not drawn to scale.

GO ON TO THE NEXT PAGE.

USE THIS SPACE FOR FIGURING.

23. Find the value of the expression: $2 \cdot |15 - 7| - 3$
    - (A) 10
    - (B) 13
    - (C) 19
    - (D) 20
    - (E) 41

24. A certain machine processes 500 letters every six minutes. At that rate, how long will it take the machine to process 7,750 letters?
    - (A) 1 hour 33 minutes
    - (B) 1 hour 39 minutes
    - (C) 1 hour 45 minutes
    - (D) 2 hours 58 minutes
    - (E) 15 hours 30 minutes

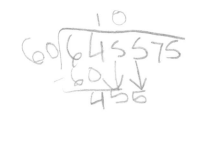

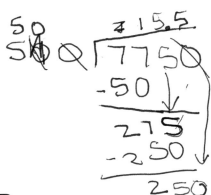

25. In the figure, $x =$
    - (A) 40
    - (B) 50
    - (C) 80
    - (D) 100
    - (E) 160

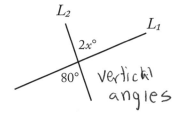

STOP
IF YOU FINISH BEFORE TIME IS CALLED,
YOU MAY CHECK YOUR WORK ON THIS SECTION ONLY.
DO NOT TURN TO ANY OTHER SECTION IN THE TEST.

Evaluating Your Middle Level SSAT

How Did You Do?

When you have completed the sample test, give yourself a pat on the back, and then take a few moments to think about your performance.

- Did you leave many questions unanswered?
- Did you run out of time?
- Did you read the directions carefully?

Based on your understanding of how well you performed, review the particular test sections that gave you difficulty. Remember, the sample tests are only used for practice.

Scoring the Practice Test

In order to compute your scores from the sample tests, you begin by calculating your "raw score" (right, wrong, and omitted answers) for each test section, using the answer keys on pages 136-141. After you have completed this task, you determine your estimated SSAT percentiles using the tables provided on page 142. The *Official Guide to the Middle Level SSAT* contains practice tests, not "retired" forms of the test. Therefore, there are no norms associated with these forms and calculations of scaled scores or specific percentile rankings are not possible. These tests are intended to familiarize you with the format, content, and timing of the test and to approximate a potential percentile rank based on a large pool of past test takers.

Computing Your Raw Score

1. Using the Practice Test Answer Keys found on pages 136-141, check your answer sheet against the list of correct answers beginning with the first Quantitative Section.

2. Mark your answer for each test question in the "Your Answer" column. Next, give yourself a ✓ in the "C" column for each correct answer, a **0** for each wrong answer in the "W" column, and a—for each question omitted in the "O" column.

Correct Answer	Your Answer	C ✓	W 0	O –
Section 1				
1. A	A	✓		
2. B	C		0	
3. C				–
4. C	C	✓		
5. D	D	✓		

3. Add the total number of correct answers and enter the number in the "Total # Correct" box; add the number of **0**s and enter in the "Total # Wrong" box. (It is not necessary to add the number of omits. You can use that information to go back and review those questions and to make sure that you understand all answers.)

4. Raw scores are calculated by using the following system:

- One point is given for each correct answer.

- No points are added or subtracted for questions omitted.

- One-fourth of a point is subtracted from the number of correct answers for each incorrect answer.

- Scores involving fractions are rounded to the nearest whole number; e.g., if the fraction is less than $\frac{1}{2}$, the number is rounded down; if the fraction is $\frac{1}{2}$ or greater, the number is rounded up.

5. Divide the number of wrong answers in the "Total # Wrong" box by 4 and enter the number in the "# Wrong ÷ 4" box. For example, if you had 32 right and 19 wrong, then your raw score is 32 minus one fourth of 19, which equals $27\frac{1}{4}$ $(32 - 4\frac{3}{4} = 27\frac{1}{4})$. If your answer contains a fraction that is less than $\frac{1}{2}$, round the number down to the nearest whole number; if the fraction is $\frac{1}{2}$ or greater, round up to the nearest whole number.

Total # Correct:

Total # Wrong:

Wrong ÷ 4:

Box 1 - Box 2:

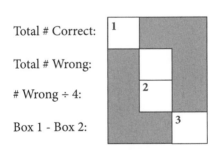

6. Add the totals of Boxes 3, 6, and 9 and enter the Raw Score for the section in the appropriate box.

Raw Score:
Add Boxes 3, 6, 9

7. Using the estimated percentile table on page 142, determine your estimated SSAT Percentile and enter this information on your worksheet.

8. Repeat this procedure for each simulated test section that you have taken.

Answer Key

Middle Level Practice Test 1 : QUANTITATIVE (Sections 1 and 4)

For each question, mark ✓ if correct (C), **0** if wrong (W), or − if omitted (O).

Correct Answer	Your Answer	C ✓	W 0	O −
Section 1				
1. A				
2. B				
3. A				
4. D				
5. B				
6. A				
7. E				
8. E				
9. A				
10. D				
11. E				
12. C				
13. E				
14. D				
15. B				
16. C				
17. D				

Correct Answer	Your Answer	C ✓	W 0	O −
18. E				
19. A				
20. E				
21. D				
22. D				
23. B				
24. E				
25. A				
Section 4				
1. E				
2. B				
3. C				
4. C				
5. E				
6. A				
7. D				
8. E				

Correct Answer	Your Answer	C ✓	W 0	O −
9. B				
10. C				
11. D				
12. D				
13. C				
14. D				
15. E				
16. C				
17. A				
18. B				
19. A				
20. A				
21. D				
22. E				
23. A				
24. B				
25. C				

Total # Correct: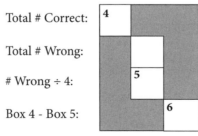

Total # Wrong:

Wrong ÷ 4:

Box 1 - Box 2:

Total # Correct: **4**

Total # Wrong:

Wrong ÷ 4: **5**

Box 4 - Box 5: **6**

Total # Correct: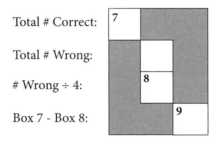

Total # Wrong:

Wrong ÷ 4:

Box 7 - Box 8:

Quantitative Raw Score:
Add Boxes 3, 6, 9

Quantitative SSAT Percentile:
See Table on page 142

Answer Key

Middle Level Practice Test I : READING (Section 2)

For each question, mark ✓ if correct (C), **0** if wrong (W), or – if omitted (O).

Correct Answer	Your Answer	C ✓	W 0	O –
1. E				
2. E				
3. A				
4. D				
5. B				
6. D				
7. A				
8. A				
9. D				
10. C				
11. B				
12. A				
13. C				
14. E				

Correct Answer	Your Answer	C ✓	W 0	O –
15. B				
16. B				
17. B				
18. C				
19. C				
20. D				
21. E				
22. D				
23. C				
24. B				
25. C				
26. E				
27. D				
28. A				

Correct Answer	Your Answer	C ✓	W 0	O –
29. D				
30. C				
31. A				
32. A				
33. E				
34. A				
35. B				
36. E				
37. C				
38. A				
39. C				
40. E				

Total # Correct: **1**

Total # Wrong: **2**

Wrong ÷ 4:

Box 1 - Box 2:   **3**

Total # Correct: **4**

Total # Wrong: **5**

Wrong ÷ 4:

Box 4 - Box 5:   **6**

Total # Correct: **7**

Total # Wrong: **8**

Wrong ÷ 4:

Box 7 - Box 8:   **9**

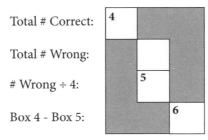

Reading Raw Score: [ ]
Add Boxes 3, 6, 9

Reading SSAT Percentile: [ ]
See Table on page 142

Answer Key

Middle Level Practice Test I : VERBAL (Section 3)

For each question, mark ✓ if correct (C), **0** if wrong (W), or – if omitted (O).

Correct Answer	Your Answer	C ✓	W **0**	O –
1. E				
2. B				
3. A				
4. D				
5. A				
6. C				
7. A				
8. B				
9. E				
10. D				
11. C				
12. D				
13. C				
14. A				
15. E				
16. B				
17. D				
18. A				
19. D				
20. A				

Correct Answer	Your Answer	C ✓	W **0**	O –
21. D				
22. A				
23. B				
24. E				
25. D				
26. E				
27. A				
28. E				
29. A				
30. A				
31. B				
32. C				
33. A				
34. C				
35. A				
36. E				
37. D				
38. A				
39. B				
40. A				

Correct Answer	Your Answer	C ✓	W **0**	O –
41. D				
42. E				
43. B				
44. D				
45. C				
46. A				
47. A				
48. E				
49. E				
50. B				
51. C				
52. A				
53. A				
54. B				
55. E				
56. B				
57. D				
58. E				
59. A				
60. E				

Total # Correct: **1**

Total # Wrong:

Wrong ÷ 4: **2**

Box 1 - Box 2: **3**

Total # Correct: **4**

Total # Wrong:

Wrong ÷ 4: **5**

Box 4 - Box 5: **6**

Total # Correct: **7**

Total # Wrong:

Wrong ÷ 4: **8**

Box 7 - Box 8: **9**

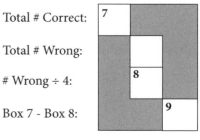

Verbal Raw Score:
Add Boxes 3, 6, 9

Verbal SSAT Percentile:
See Table on page 142

Answer Key

Middle Level Practice Test II : QUANTITATIVE (Sections 1 and 4)

For each question, mark ✓ if correct (C), **0** if wrong (W), or − if omitted (O).

Correct Answer	Your Answer	C ✓	W 0	O −
Section 1				
1. D				
2. C				
3. B				
4. A				
5. B				
6. C				
7. C				
8. B				
9. A				
10. D				
11. D				
12. B				
13. B				
14. E				
15. A				
16. E				
17. B				

Correct Answer	Your Answer	C ✓	W 0	O −
18. B				
19. E				
20. D				
21. C				
22. C				
23. A				
24. D				
25. D				
Section 4				
1. C				
2. B				
3. B				
4. A				
5. D				
6. B				
7. D				
8. E				

Correct Answer	Your Answer	C ✓	W 0	O −
9. D				
10. D				
11. E				
12. A				
13. E				
14. C				
15. D				
16. A				
17. C				
18. B				
19. A				
20. B				
21. A				
22. B				
23. B				
24. A				
25. A				

Total # Correct:

Total # Wrong:

Wrong ÷ 4:

Box 1 - Box 2:

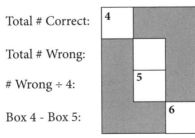

Total # Correct:

Total # Wrong:

Wrong ÷ 4:

Box 4 - Box 5:

Total # Correct:

Total # Wrong:

Wrong ÷ 4:

Box 7 - Box 8:

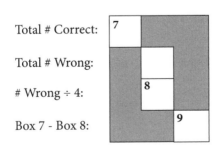

Quantitative Raw Score:
Add Boxes 3, 6, 9

Quantitative SSAT Percentile:
See Table on page 142

Answer Key

Middle Level Practice Test II : READING (Section 2)

For each question, mark ✓ if correct (C), **0** if wrong (W), or − if omitted (O).

Correct Answer	Your Answer	C ✓	W 0	O −
1. C				
2. C				
3. E				
4. D				
5. C				
6. A				
7. D				
8. A				
9. B				
10. B				
11. E				
12. E				
13. B				
14. A				

Correct Answer	Your Answer	C ✓	W 0	O −
15. C				
16. E				
17. C				
18. B				
19. A				
20. E				
21. E				
22. B				
23. A				
24. E				
25. A				
26. E				
27. D				
28. A				

Correct Answer	Your Answer	C ✓	W 0	O −
29. C				
30. A				
31. D				
32. A				
33. D				
34. D				
35. A				
36. B				
37. D				
38. D				
39. C				
40. C				

Total # Correct: **1**

Total # Wrong:

Wrong ÷ 4: **2**

Box 1 - Box 2: **3**

Total # Correct: **4**

Total # Wrong:

Wrong ÷ 4: **5**

Box 4 - Box 5: **6**

Total # Correct: **7**

Total # Wrong:

Wrong ÷ 4: **8**

Box 7 - Box 8: **9**

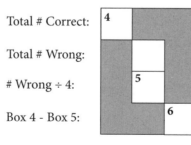

Reading Raw Score:
Add Boxes 3, 6, 9

Reading SSAT Percentile:
See Table on page 142

Answer Key

Middle Level Practice Test II : VERBAL (Section 3)

For each question, mark ✓ if correct (C), **0** if wrong (W), or – if omitted (O).

Correct Answer	Your Answer	C ✓	W 0	O –
1. C				
2. C				
3. D				
4. C				
5. D				
6. B				
7. D				
8. C				
9. A				
10. C				
11. A				
12. B				
13. E				
14. E				
15. A				
16. C				
17. E				
18. A				
19. E				
20. B				

Correct Answer	Your Answer	C ✓	W 0	O –
21. C				
22. D				
23. A				
24. D				
25. B				
26. D				
27. C				
28. A				
29. B				
30. B				
31. A				
32. B				
33. A				
34. C				
35. D				
36. C				
37. B				
38. C				
39. D				
40. D				

Correct Answer	Your Answer	C ✓	W 0	O –
41. A				
42. B				
43. A				
44. E				
45. C				
46. E				
47. B				
48. E				
49. B				
50. C				
51. B				
52. A				
53. C				
54. E				
55. A				
56. A				
57. B				
58. B				
59. C				
60. A				

Total # Correct: 1
Total # Wrong:
Wrong ÷ 4: 2
Box 1 - Box 2: 3

Total # Correct: 4
Total # Wrong:
Wrong ÷ 4: 5
Box 4 - Box 5: 6

Total # Correct: 7
Total # Wrong:
Wrong ÷ 4: 8
Box 7 - Box 8: 9

Verbal Raw Score:
Add Boxes 3, 6, 9

Verbal SSAT Percentile:
See Table on page 142

Interpreting Your Scores — Percentiles

Your official SSAT score report will include a measure of your scores against all students of your gender and grade who have taken the SSAT in the U.S. and Canada for the first time on one of the eight Standard test dates in the past three years (SSAT Percentile).

Because the *Official Guide to the Middle Level SSAT* guide contains practice tests and not "retired" forms of the test, there are no norms associated with these forms and calculations of scaled scores or specific percentile rankings are not possible, but the following charts will give you a good estimate of where your scores would fall. These tests are intended to familiarize you with the format, content, and timing of the test and to approximate a potential percentile rank based on a large pool of past test takers.

Table: Middle Level Estimated SSAT Percentiles			
Raw Score	Verbal Percentile	Quantitative Percentile	Reading Percentile
60	99		
55	99		
50	97	99	
45	93	93	
40	85	80	99
35	75	65	96
30	62	50	82
25	47	36	63
20	31	23	43
15	18	13	24
10	8	6	11
5	2	2	3
0	1	1	1
-5	1	1	1
-10 and lower	1	1	1

Notes

Notes